Manifest

der

Kommunistischen Partei.

———

Veröffentlicht im Februar 1848.

———

London.
Gedruckt in der Office der „Bildungs-Gesellschaft für Arbeiter"
von J. E. Burghard.
46, LIVERPOOL STREET, BISHOPSGATE.

>>MANIFEST<<
www.46LiverpoolSt.org

ISBN 1-870736-48-6

Published by Working Press
with support from The Barry Amiel & Norman Melburn Trust
with thanks to Stiftung Archiv der Parteien und Massenorganisationen der DDR
im Bundesarchiv
Printed by Spider Web

publication: anti-copyright @ 1999 Tim Brennan & Geoff Cox
http://www.46LiverpoolSt.org
software: copyleft © 1999 Adrian Ward/Sidestream
http://www.sidestream.org

Working Press
47 Melbourne Avenue
Palmers Green
London N13 4SY

Manifest™ v1.0 README

www.46LiverpoolSt.org

'Manifest der Kommunistischen Partei' was first printed as a pamphlet in February 1848, in the office of the Workers' Educational Association (Communistischer Arbeiterbildungsverein), 46 Liverpool Street, Bishopsgate, London. A facsimile of this first edition in German is reprinted in this publication alongside the most commonly published English translation of 1888, viewed through our 'Manifest' software. To download and for further information, visit the website http://www.46LiverpoolSt.org and read on.

Technical information:
The 'Manifest' software does not require any special installation requirements, simply install it on your hard drive as an alternative to your usual web browser. It will allow you to browse the web but reads text-only files. Once activated, the Manifest software not only enables the user to browse but simultaneously distributes information by running as a web server. In this way visitors to your machine will be able to browse through the text-only contents of your hard disk. A list of machines that can be browsed can be obtained by visiting the 46LiverpoolSt.org website. For security reasons, the Manifest web server component does not support binary file transfers or any form of CGI interface, including GET/POST requests or file uploads. Files on the local machine cannot be changed by the web server, but can only read. We encourage you to run your own web server using one of the many free httpd programs available if you wish to provide a more complete service. For the web server component to be able to handle requests properly, it must not be restricted by a firewall or proxy system.

'Manifest' is available for Macintosh PowerPC and for Windows.
Mac version:
MacOS 7.5 or higher on a PowerPC Macintosh.
Working internet/dialup connection with fully configured TCP/IP settings.
Open Transport.
At least 6 megabytes of available memory.
A hard disk with at least 2 megabytes of free space available.
PC version:
Microsoft Windows 95, 98 or NT.
Working internet/dialup connection with fully configured TCP/IP network protocol.
At least 8 megabytes of available memory.
A hard disk with at least 2 megabytes of free space available.

Distribution:
This software may not, under any circumstances, be distributed as commercial software, in exchange for money or cash alternatives. It is distributed as freeware, and is released under the GNU General Public License agreement (version 2, 1991) which stipulates that the software source code must remain freely available, and that anyone may copy and modify it as they wish, subject to the terms and conditions contained in the License agreement.

For further details on this, turn to the endpages and/or visit http://www.46LiverpoolSt.org

Manifesto

of the

Communist Party.

A spectre is haunting Europe -- the spectre of communism. All the
powers of old Europe have entered into a holy alliance to exorcise this
spectre: Pope and Tsar, Metternich and Guizot, French Radicals and
German police-spies.
Where is the party in opposition that has not been decried as
communistic by its opponents in power? Where is the opposition that
has not hurled back the branding reproach of communism, against the
more advanced opposition parties, as well as against its reactionary
adversaries?
Two things result from this fact:
I. Communism is already acknowledged by all European powers to be
itself a power.
II. It is high time that Communists should openly, in the face of the
whole world, publish their views, their aims, their tendencies, and
meet this nursery tale of the spectre of communism with a manifesto of
the party itself.
To this end, Communists of various nationalities have assembled in
London and sketched the following manifesto, to be published in
the English, French, German, Italian, Flemish and Danish languages.

I.

Bourgeois and Proletarians

The history of all hitherto existing society is the history of class
struggles.
Freeman and slave, patrician and plebian, lord and serf, guild-master
and journeyman, in a word, oppressor and oppressed, stood in constant
opposition to one another, carried on an uninterrupted, now hidden,
now open fight, a fight that each time ended, either in a
revolutionary reconstitution of society at large, or in the common
ruin of the contending classes.
In the earlier epochs of history, we find almost everywhere a
complicated arrangement of society into various orders, a manifold
gradation of social rank. In ancient Rome we have pa-

Manifest

der

Kommunistischen Partei.

Ein Gespenst geht um in Europa—das Gespenst des Kommunismus. Alle Mächte des alten Europa haben sich zu einer heiligen Hetzjagd gegen dies Gespenst verbündet, der Papst und der Czar, Metternich und Guizot, französische Radikale und deutsche Polizisten.

Wo ist die Oppositionspartei, die nicht von ihren regierenden Gegnern als kommunistisch verschrieen worden wäre, wo die Oppositionspartei, die den fortgeschritteneren Oppositionsleuten sowohl, wie ihren reaktionären Gegnern den brandmarkenden Vorwurf des Kommunismus nicht zurückgeschleudert hätte?

Zweierlei geht aus dieser Thatsache hervor.

Der Kommunismus wird bereits von allen europäischen Mächten als eine Macht anerkannt.

Es ist hohe Zeit daß die Kommunisten ihre Anschauungsweise, ihre Zwecke, ihre Tendenzen vor der ganzen Welt offen darlegen, und den Mährchen vom Gespenst des Kommunismus ein Manifest der Partei selbst entgegenstellen.

Zu diesem Zweck haben sich Kommunisten der verschiedensten Nationalität in London versammelt und das folgende Manifest entworfen, das in englischer, französischer, deutscher, italienischer, flämmischer und dänischer Sprache veröffentlicht wird.

I.

Bourgeois und Proletarier.

Die Geschichte aller bisherigen Gesellschaft ist die Geschichte von Klassenkämpfen.

Freier und Sklave, Patrizier und Plebejer, Baron und Leibeigner, Zunftbürger und Gesell, kurz, Unterdrücker und Unterdrückte standen in stetem Gegensatz zu einander, führten einen ununterbrochenen, bald versteckten bald offenen Kampf, einen Kampf, der jedesmal mit einer revolutionären Umgestaltung der ganzen Gesellschaft endete, oder mit dem gemeinsamen Untergang der kämpfenden Klassen.

In den früheren Epochen der Geschichte finden wir fast überall eine vollständige Gliederung der Gesellschaft in verschiedene Stände, eine mannichfaltige Abstufung der gesellschaftlichen Stellungen. Im alten Rom haben wir Patrizier, Ritter, Plebejer, Sklaven; im Mittelalter Feudalherren, Vasallen, Zunftbürger, Gesellen, Leibeigene, und noch dazu in fast jeder dieser Klassen wieder besondere Abstufungen.

Die aus dem Untergange der feudalen Gesellschaft hervorgegangene moderne bürgerliche Gesellschaft hat die Klassengegensätze nicht aufgehoben. Sie hat nur neue Klassen, neue Bedingungen der Unterdrückung, neue Gestaltungen des Kampfes an die Stelle der alten gesetzt.

Unsere Epoche, die Epoche der Bourgeoisie, zeichnet sich jedoch dadurch aus, daß sie die Klassengegensätze vereinfacht hat. Die ganze Gesellschaft spaltet sich mehr und mehr in zwei große feindliche Lager, in zwei große einander direkt gegenüberstehende Klassen—Bourgeoisie and Proletariat.

Aus den Leibeigenen des Mittelalters gingen die Pfahlbürger der ersten Städte hervor; aus dieser Pfahlbürgerschaft entwickelten sich die ersten Elemente der Bourgeoisie.

Die Entdeckung Amerika's, die Umschiffung Afrika's schufen der aufkommenden Bourgeoisie ein neues Terrain. Der ostindische und chinesische Markt, die Kolonisirung von Amerika, der Austausch mit den Kolonien, die Vermehrung der Tauschmittel und der Waaren überhaupt gaben dem Handel, der Schifffahrt, der Industrie einen niegekannten Aufschwung, und damit dem revolutionären Element in der zerfallenden feudalen Gesellschaft eine rasche Entwicklung.

Die bisherige feudale oder zünftige Betriebsweise der Industrie reichte nicht mehr aus für den mit den neuen Märkten anwachsenden Bedarf. Die Manufaktur trat an ihre Stelle. Die Zunftmeister wurden verdrängt durch den industriellen Mittelstand; die Theilung der Arbeit zwischen den verschiedenen Corporationen verschwand vor der Theilung der Arbeit in der einzelnen Werkstatt selbst.

Aber immer wuchsen die Märkte, immer stieg der Bedarf. Auch die Manufaktur reichte nicht mehr aus. Da revolutionirten der Dampf und die Maschinerie die industrielle Produktion. An die Stelle der Manufaktur trat die moderne große Industrie, an die Stelle des industriellen Mittelstandes traten die industriellen Millionäre, die Chefs ganzer industriellen Armeen, die modernen Bourgeois.

Die große Industrie hat den Weltmarkt hergestellt, den die Entdeckung Amerika's vorbereitete. Der Weltmarkt hat dem Handel, der Schifffahrt, den Landkommunikationen eine unermeßliche Entwicklung gegeben. Diese hat wieder auf die Ausdehnung der Industrie zurückgewirkt, und in demselben Maße, worin Industrie, Handel, Schifffahrt, Eisenbahnen sich ausdehnten, in demselben Maße entwickelte sich die Bourgeoisie, vermehrte sie ihre Kapitalien, drängte sie alle vom Mittelalter her überlieferten Klassen in den Hintergrund.

Wir sehen also wie die moderne Bourgeoisie selbst das Produkt eines langen Entwicklungsganges, einer Reihe von Umwälzungen in der Produktions- und Verkehrsweise ist.

Jede dieser Entwicklungsstufen der Bourgeoisie war begleitet von einem entsprechenden politischen Fortschritt. Unterdrückter Stand unter der Herrschaft der Feudalherren, bewaffnete und sich selbst verwaltende Associationen in der Commune, hier unabhängige städtische Republik, dort dritter steuerpflichtiger Stand der Monarchie, dann zur Zeit der Manufaktur Gegengewicht gegen den Adel in der ständischen oder in der absoluten Monarchie und Hauptgrundlage der großen Monarchien überhaupt, erkämpfte sie sich endlich seit der Herstellung der großen Industrie und des Weltmarktes im modernen Repräsentativstaat die ausschließliche politische Herrschaft. Die moderne Staatsgewalt ist nur ein Ausschuß, der die gemeinschaftlichen Geschäfte der ganzen Bourgeoisklasse verwaltet.

-tricians, knights, plebians, slaves; in the Middle Ages, feudal lords, vassals, guild-masters, journeymen, apprentices, serfs; in almost all of these classes, again, subordinate gradations.

The modern bourgeois society that has sprouted from the ruins of feudal society has not done away with class antagonisms. It has but established new classes, new conditions of oppression, new forms of struggle in place of the old ones.

Our epoch, the epoch of the bourgeoisie, possesses, however, this distinct feature: it has simplified class antagonisms. Society as a whole is more and more splitting up into two great hostile camps, into two great classes directly facing each other -- bourgeoisie and proletariat.

From the serfs of the Middle Ages sprang the chartered burghers of the earliest towns. From these burgesses the first elements of the bourgeoisie were developed.

The discovery of America, the rounding of the Cape, opened up fresh ground for the rising bourgeoisie. The East-Indian and Chinese markets, the colonisation of America, trade with the colonies, the increase in the means of exchange and in commodities generally, gave to commerce, to navigation, to industry, an impulse never before known, and thereby, to the revolutionary element in the tottering feudal society, a rapid development.

The feudal system of industry, in which industrial production was monopolised by closed guilds, now no longer suffices for the growing wants of the new markets. The manufacturing system took its place. The guild-masters were pushed aside by the manufacturing middle class; division of labour between the different corporate guilds vanished in the face of division of labour in each single workshop.

Meantime, the markets kept ever growing, the demand ever rising. Even manufacturers no longer sufficed. Thereupon, steam and machinery revolutionised industrial production. The place of manufacture was taken by the giant, Modern Industry; the place of the industrial middle class by industrial millionaires, the leaders of the whole industrial armies, the modern bourgeois.

Modern industry has established the world market, for which the discovery of America paved the way. This market has given an immense development to commerce, to navigation, to communication by land. This development has, in turn, reacted on the extension of industry; and in proportion as industry, commerce, navigation, railways extended, in the same proportion the bourgeoisie developed, increased its capital, and pushed into the background every class handed down from the Middle Ages.

We see, therefore, how the modern bourgeoisie is itself the product of a long course of development, of a series of revolutions in the modes of production and of exchange.

Each step in the development of the bourgeoisie was accompanied by a corresponding political advance in that class. An oppressed class under the sway of the feudal nobility, an armed and self-governing association of medieval commune: here independent urban republic (as in Italy and Germany); there taxable "third estate" of the monarchy (as in France); afterward, in the period of manufacturing proper, serving either the semi-feudal or the absolute monarchy as a counterpoise against the nobility, and, in fact, cornerstone of the great monarchies in general -- the bourgeoisie has at last, since the establishment of Modern Industry and of the world market, conquered for itself, in the modern representative state, exclusive political sway. The executive of the modern state is but a committee for managing the common affairs of the whole bourgeoisie.

Back Forward Reload Stop

URL: http://www.46liverpoolst.org/manifest/05.html

The bourgeoisie, historically, has played a most revolutionary part. The bourgeoisie, wherever it has got the upper hand, has put an end to all feudal, patriarchal, idyllic relations. It has pitilessly torn asunder the motley feudal ties that bound man to his "natural superiors", and has left no other nexus between man and man than naked self-interest, than callous "cash payment". It has drowned out the most heavenly ecstacies of religious fervour, of chivalrous enthusiasm, of philistine sentimentalism, in the icy water of egotistical calculation. It has resolved personal worth into exchange value, and in place of the numberless indefeasible chartered freedoms, has set up that single, unconscionable freedom -- Free Trade. In one word, for exploitation, veiled by religious and political illusions, it has substituted naked, shameless, direct, brutal exploitation. The bourgeoisie has stripped of its halo every occupation hitherto honoured and looked up to with reverent awe. It has converted the physician, the lawyer, the priest, the poet, the man of science, into its paid wage labourers.
The bourgeoisie has torn away from the family its sentimental veil, and has reduced the family relation into a mere money relation. The bourgeoisie has disclosed how it came to pass that the brutal display of vigour in the Middle Ages, which reactionaries so much admire, found its fitting complement in the most slothful indolence. It has been the first to show what man's activity can bring about. It has accomplished wonders far surpassing Egyptian pyramids, Roman aqueducts, and Gothic cathedrals; it has conducted expeditions that put in the shade all former exoduses of nations and crusades. The bourgeoisie cannot exist without constantly revolutionising the instruments of production, and thereby the relations of production, and with them the whole relations of society. Conservation of the old modes of production in unaltered form, was, on the contrary, the first condition of existence for all earlier industrial classes. Constant revolutionising of production, uninterrupted disturbance of all social conditions, everlasting uncertainty and agitation distinguish the bourgeois epoch from all earlier ones. All fixed, fast frozen relations, with their train of ancient and venerable prejudices and opinions, are swept away, all new-formed ones become antiquated before they can ossify. All that is solid melts into air, all that is holy is profaned, and man is at last compelled to face with sober senses his real condition of life and his relations with his kind.
The need of a constantly expanding market for its products chases the bourgeoisie over the entire surface of the globe. It must nestle everywhere, settle everywhere, establish connections everywhere. The bourgeoisie has, through its exploitation of the world market, given a cosmopolitan character to production and consumption in every country. To the great chagrin of reactionaries, it has drawn from under the feet of industry the national ground on which it stood. All old-established national industries have been destroyed or are daily being destroyed. They are dislodged by new industries, whose introduction becomes a life and death question for all civilised nations, by industries that no longer work up indigenous raw material, but raw material drawn from the remotest zones; industries whose products are consumed, not only at home, but in every quarter of the globe. In place of the old wants, satisfied by the production of the country, we find new wants, requiring for their satisfaction the products of distant lands and climes. In place of the old local and national seclusion and self-sufficiency, we have intercourse

Die Bourgeoisie hat in der Geschichte eine höchst revolutionäre Rolle gespielt.

Die Bourgeoisie, wo sie zur Herrschaft gekommen, hat alle feudalen, patriarchalischen, idyllischen Verhältnisse zerstört. Sie hat die buntscheckigen Feudalbande, die den Menschen an seinen natürlichen Vorgesetzten knüpften, unbarmherzig zerrissen, und kein anderes Band zwischen Mensch und Mensch übrig gelassen, als das nackte Interesse, als die gefühllose „baare Zahlung." Sie hat die heiligen Schauer der frommen Schwärmerei, der ritterlichen Begeisterung, der spießbürgerlichen Wehmuth in dem eiskalten Wasser egoistischer Berechnung ertränkt. Sie hat die persönliche Würde in den Tauschwerth aufgelöst, und an die Stelle der zahllosen verbrieften und wohlerworbenen Freiheiten die Eine gewissenlose Handelsfreiheit gesetzt. Sie hat, mit einem Wort, an die Stelle der mit religiösen und politischen Illusionen verhüllten Ausbeutung die offene, unverschämte, direkte, dürre Ausbeutung gesetzt.

Die Bourgeoisie hat alle bisher ehrwürdigen und mit frommer Scheu betrachteten Thätigkeiten ihres Heiligenscheins entkleidet. Sie hat den Arzt, den Juristen, den Pfaffen, den Poeten, den Mann der Wissenschaft in ihre bezahlten Lohnarbeiter verwandelt.

Die Bourgeoisie hat dem Familienverhältniß seinen rührend-sentimentalen Schleier abgerissen und es auf ein reines Geldverhältniß zurückgeführt.

Die Bourgeoisie hat enthüllt wie die brutale Kraftäußerung, die die Reaktion so sehr am Mittelalter bewundert, in der trägsten Bärenhäuterei ihre passende Ergänzung fand. Erst sie hat bewiesen was die Thätigkeit der Menschen zu Stande bringen kann. Sie hat ganz andere Wunderwerke vollbracht als egyptische Pyramiden, römische Wasserleitungen und gothische Kathedralen, sie hat ganz andere Züge ausgeführt, als Völkerwanderungen und Kreuzzüge.

Die Bourgeoisie kann nicht existiren ohne die Produktionsinstrumente, also die Produktionsverhältnisse, also sämmtliche gesellschaftlichen Verhältnisse fortwährend zu revolutioniren. Unveränderte Beibehaltung der alten Produktionsweise war dagegen die erste Existenzbedingung aller früheren industriellen Klassen. Die fortwährende Umwälzung der Produktion, die ununterbrochene Erschütterung aller gesellschaftlichen Zustände, die ewige Unsicherheit und Bewegung zeichnet die Bourgeois-Epoche vor allen früheren aus. Alle festen, eingerosteten Verhältnisse mit ihrem Gefolge von altehrwürdigen Vorstellungen und Anschauungen werden aufgelöst, alle neugebildeten veralten, ehe sie verknöchern können. Alles Ständische und Stehende verdampft, alles Heilige wird entweiht, und die Menschen sind endlich gezwungen, ihre Lebensstellung, ihre gegenseitigen Beziehungen mit nüchternen Augen anzusehen.

Das Bedürfniß nach einem stets ausgedehnteren Absatz für ihre Produkte jagt die Bourgeoisie über die ganze Erdkugel. Ueberall muß sie sich einnisten, überall anbauen, überall Verbindungen herstellen.

Die Bourgeoisie hat durch die Exploitation des Weltmarkts die Produktion und Konsumtion aller Länder kosmopolitisch gestaltet. Sie hat zum großen Bedauern der Reaktionäre den nationalen Boden der Industrie unter den Füßen weggezogen. Die uralten nationalen Industrieen sind vernichtet worden und werden noch täglich vernichtet. Sie werden verdrängt durch neue Industrieen, deren Einführung eine Lebensfrage für alle civilisirte Nationen wird, durch Industrieen, die nicht mehr einheimische Rohstoffe, sondern den entlegensten Zonen angehörige Rohstoffe verarbeiten, und deren Fabrikate nicht nur im Lande selbst, sondern in allen Weltheilen zugleich verbraucht werden. An die Stelle der alten, durch Landeserzeugnisse befriedigten Bedürfnisse treten neue, welche die Produkte der entferntesten Länder und Klimate zu ihrer Befriedigung erheischen. An die Stelle der alten lokalen und nationalen Selbstgenügsamkeit und Abgeschlossenheit tritt ein allseitiger Verkehr, eine allseitige Abhängigkeit der Nationen von einander. Und wie in der materiellen, so auch in der geistigen Produktion. Die geistigen Erzeugnisse der einzelnen Nationen werden Gemeingut. Die nationale Einseitigkeit und Beschränktheit wird mehr und mehr unmöglich, und aus den vielen nationalen und lokalen Literaturen bildet sich eine Weltliteratur.

Die Bourgeoisie reißt durch die rasche Verbesserung aller Produktions-Instrumente, durch die unendlich erleichterten Kommunikationen alle, auch die barbarischsten Nationen in die Civilisation. Die wohlfeilen Preise ihrer Waaren sind die schwere Artillerie, mit der sie alle chinesischen Mauern in den Grund schießt, mit der sie den hartnäckigsten Fremdenhaß der Barbaren zur Kapitulation zwingt. Sie zwingt alle Nationen die Produktionsweise der Bourgeoisie sich anzueignen, wenn sie nicht zu Grunde gehen wollen; sie zwingt sie die sogenannte Civilisation bei sich selbst einzuführen, d. h. Bourgeois zu werden. Mit einem Wort, sie schafft sich eine Welt nach ihrem eigenen Bilde.

Die Bourgeoisie hat das Land der Herrschaft der Stadt unterworfen. Sie hat enorme Städte geschaffen, sie hat die Zahl der städtischen Bevölkerung gegenüber der ländlichen in hohem Grade vermehrt, und so einen bedeutenden Theil der Bevölkerung dem Idiotismus des Landlebens entrissen. Wie sie das Land von der Stadt, hat sie die barbarischen und halbbarbarischen Länder von den civilisirten, die Bauernvölker von den Bourgeoisvölkern, den Orient vom Occident abhängig gemacht.

Die Bourgeoisie hebt mehr und mehr die Zersplitterung der Produktionsmittel, des Besitzes und der Bevölkerung auf. Sie hat die Bevölkerung agglomerirt, die Produktionsmittel centralisirt und das Eigenthum in wenigen Händen koncentrirt. Die nothwendige Folge hiervon war die politische Centralisation. Unabhängige, fast nur verbündete Provinzen mit verschiedenen Interessen, Gesetzen, Regierungen und Zöllen wurden zusammengedrängt in Eine Nation, Eine Regierung, Ein Gesetz, Ein nationales Klasseninteresse, Eine Douanenlinie.

Die Bourgeoisie hat in ihrer kaum hundertjährigen Klassenherrschaft massenhaftere und kolossalere Produktionskräfte geschaffen als alle vergangenen Generationen zusammen. Unterjochung der Naturkräfte, Maschinerie, Anwendung der Chemie auf Industrie und Ackerbau, Dampfschifffahrt, Eisenbahnen, elektrische Telegraphen, Urbarmachung ganzer Welttheile, Schiffbarmachung der Flüsse, ganze aus dem Boden hervorgestampfte Bevölkerungen—welch früheres Jahrhundert ahnte, daß solche Produktionskräfte im Schooß der gesellschaftlichen Arbeit schlummerten.

Wir haben aber gesehen: Die Produktions- und Verkehrsmittel, auf deren Grundlage sich die Bourgeoisie heranbildete, wurden in der feudalen Gesellschaft erzeugt. Auf einer gewissen Stufe der Entwicklung dieser Produktions- und Verkehrsmittel entsprachen die Verhältnisse, worin die feudale Gesellschaft producirte und austauschte, die feudale Organisation der Agrikultur und Manufaktur, mit einem Wort die feudalen Eigenthums-Verhältnisse den schon entwickelten Produktivkräften nicht mehr. Sie hemmten die Produktion statt sie zu fördern. Sie verwandelten sich in eben so viele Fesseln. Sie mußten gesprengt werden, sie wurden gesprengt.

An ihre Stelle trat die freie Konkurrenz mit der ihr angemessenen gesellschaftlichen und politischen Konstitution, mit der ökonomischen und politischen Herrschaft der Bourgeois-Klasse.

Unter unsren Augen geht eine ähnliche Bewegung vor. Die bürgerlichen Produktions- und Verkehrs-Verhältnisse, die bürgerlichen Eigenthums-Verhältnisse, die moderne bürgerliche Gesellschaft, die so gewaltige Produktions- und Verkehrsmittel hervorgezaubert hat, gleicht dem Hexenmeister, der die unterirdischen Gewalten nicht mehr zu beherrschen vermag, die er herauf beschwor.

in every direction, universal inter-dependence of nations. And as in material, so also in intellectual production. The intellectual creations of individual nations become common property. National one-sidedness and narrow-mindedness become more and more impossible, and from the numerous national and local literatures, there arises a world literature.

The bourgeoisie, by the rapid improvement of all instruments of production, by the immensely facilitated means of communication, draws all, even the most barbarian, nations into civilisation. The cheap prices of commodities are the heavy artillery with which it forces the barbarians' intensely obstinate hatred of foreigners to capitulate. It compels all nations, on pain of extinction, to adopt the bourgeois mode of production; it compels them to introduce what it calls civilisation into their midst, i.e., to become bourgeois themselves. In one word, it creates a world after its own image.

The bourgeoisie has subjected the country to the rule of the towns. It has created enormous cities, has greatly increased the urban population as compared with the rural, and has thus rescued a considerable part of the population from the idiocy of rural life. Just as it has made the country dependent on the towns, so it has made barbarian and semi-barbarian countries dependent on the civilised ones, nations of peasants on nations of bourgeois, the East on the West.

The bourgeoisie keeps more and more doing away with the scattered state of the population, of the means of production, and of property. It has agglomerated population, centralised the means of production, and has concentrated property in a few hands. The necessary consequence of this was political centralisation. Independent, or but loosely connected provinces, with separate interests, laws, governments, and systems of taxation, became lumped together into one nation, with one government, one code of laws, one national class interest, one frontier, and one customs tariff.

The bourgeoisie, during its rule of scarce one hundred years, has created more massive and more colossal productive forces than have all preceding generations together. Subjection of nature's forces to man, machinery, application of chemistry to industry and agriculture, steam navigation, railways, electric telegraphs, clearing of whole continents for cultivation, canalisation or rivers, whole populations conjured out of the ground -- what earlier century had even a presentiment that such productive forces slumbered in the lap of social labour?

We see then: the means of production and of exchange, on whose foundation the bourgeoisie built itself up, were generated in feudal society. At a certain stage in the development of these means of production and of exchange, the conditions under which feudal society produced and exchanged, the feudal organisation of agriculture and manufacturing industry, in one word, the feudal relations of property became no longer compatible with the already developed productive forces; they became so many fetters. They had to be burst asunder; they were burst asunder.

Into their place stepped free competition, accompanied by a social and political constitution adapted in it, and the economic and political sway of the bourgeois class.

A similar movement is going on before our own eyes. Modern bourgeois society, with its relations of production, of exchange and of property, a society that has conjured up such gigantic means of production and of exchange, is like the sorcerer who is no longer able to control the powers of the nether world whom he has called up by his spells.

URL: http://www.46liverpoolst.org/manifest/07.html

For many a decade past, the history of industry and commerce is but the history of the revolt of modern productive forces against modern conditions of production, against the property relations that are the conditions for the existence of the bourgeois and of its rule. It is enough to mention the commercial crises that, by their periodical return, put the existence of the entire bourgeois society on its trial, each time more threateningly. In these crises, a great part not only of the existing products, but also of the previously created productive forces, are periodically destroyed. In these crises, there breaks out an epidemic that, in all earlier epochs, would have seemed an absurdity -- the epidemic of over-production. Society suddenly finds itself put back into a state of momentary barbarism; it appears as if a famine, a universal war of devastation, had cut off the supply of every means of subsistence; industry and commerce seem to be destroyed. And why? Because there is too much civilisation, too much means of subsistence, too much industry, too much commerce. The productive forces at the disposal of society no longer tend to further the development of the conditions of bourgeois property; on the contrary, they have become too powerful for these conditions, by which they are fettered, and so soon as they overcome these fetters, they bring disorder into the whole of bourgeois society, endanger the existence of bourgeois property. The conditions of bourgeois society are too narrow to comprise the wealth created by them. And how does the bourgeoisie get over these crises? One the one hand, by enforced destruction of a mass of productive forces; on the other, by the conquest of new markets, and by the more thorough exploitation of the old ones. That is to say, by paving the way for more extensive and more destructive crises, and by diminishing the means whereby crises are prevented.
The weapons with which the bourgeoisie felled feudalism to the ground are now turned against the bourgeoisie itself.
But not only has the bourgeoisie forged the weapons that bring death to itself; it has also called into existence the men who are to wield those weapons -- the modern working class -- the proletarians.
In proportion as the bourgeoisie, i.e., capital, is developed, in the same proportion is the proletariat, the modern working class, developed -- a class of labourers, who live only so long as they find work, and who find work only so long as their labour increases capital. These labourers, who must sell themselves piecemeal, are a commodity, like every other article of commerce, and are consequently exposed to all the vicissitudes of competition, to all the fluctuations of the market.
Owing to the extensive use of machinery, and to the division of labour, the work of the proletarians has lost all individual character, and, consequently, all charm for the workman. He becomes an appendage of the machine, and it is only the most simple, most monotonous, and most easily acquired knack, that is required of him. Hence, the cost of production of a workman is restricted, almost entirely, to the means of subsistence that he requires for maintenance, and for the propagation of his race. But the price of a commodity, and therefore also of labour, is equal to its cost of production. In proportion, therefore, as the repulsiveness of the work increases, the wage decreases. What is more, in proportion as the use of machinery and division of labour increases, in the same proportion the burden of toil also increases, whether by prolongation of the working hours, by the increase of the work exacted in a given time, or by increased speed of machinery, etc.
Modern Industry has converted the little workshop of the patriarchal master into the great factory of the industrial capitalist. Masses of

Seit Dezennien ist die Geschichte der Industrie und des Handels nur noch die Geschichte der Empörung der modernen Produktivkräfte gegen die modernen Produktions-Verhältnisse, gegen die Eigenthums-Verhältnisse, welche die Lebens-Bedingungen der Bourgeoisie und ihrer Herrschaft sind. Es genügt die Handelskrisen zu nennen, welche in ihrer periodischen Wiederkehr immer drohender die Existenz der ganzen bürgerlichen Gesellschaft in Frage stellen. In den Handelskrisen wird ein großer Theil nicht nur der erzeugten Produkte, sondern sogar der bereits geschaffenen Produktivkräfte regelmäßig vernichtet. In der Krisen bricht eine gesellschaftliche Epidemie aus, welche allen früheren Epochen als ein Widersinn erschienen wäre—die Epidemie der Ueberproduktion. Die Gesellschaft findet sich plötzlich in einen Zustand momentaner Barbarei zurückversetzt; eine Hungersnoth, ein allgemeiner Verwüstungskrieg scheinen ihr alle Lebensmittel abgeschnitten zu haben; die Industrie, der Handel scheinen vernichtet, und warum? Weil sie zu viel Civilisation, zu viel Lebensmittel, zu viel Industrie, zu viel Handel besitzt. Die Produktivkräfte, die ihr zur Verfügung stehen, dienen nicht mehr zur Beförderung der bürgerlichen Civilisation und der bürgerlichen Eigenthums-Verhältnisse; im Gegentheil, sie sind zu gewaltig für diese Verhältnisse geworden, sie werden von ihnen gehemmt, und so bald sie dies Hemmniß überwinden, bringen sie die ganze bürgerliche Gesellschaft in Unordnung, gefährden sie die Existenz des bürgerlichen Eigenthums. Die bürgerlichen Verhältnisse sind zu eng geworden um den von ihnen erzeugten Reichthum zu fassen.—Wodurch überwindet die Bourgeoisie die Krisen? Einerseits durch die erzwungene Vernichtung einer Masse von Produktivkräften; andererseits durch die Eroberung neuer Märkte, und die gründlichere Ausbeutung der alten Märkte. Wodurch also? Dadurch, daß sie allseitigere und gewaltigere Krisen vorbereitet und die Mittel, den Krisen vorzubeugen, vermindert.

Die Waffen, womit die Bourgeoisie den Feudalismus zu Boden geschlagen hat, richten sich jetzt gegen die Bourgeoisie selbst.

Aber die Bourgeoisie hat nicht nur die Waffen geschmiedet, die ihr den Tod bringen; sie hat auch die Männer gezeugt, die diese Waffen führen werden—die modernen Arbeiter, die Proletarier.

In demselben Maße, worin sich die Bourgeoisie, d. h. das Kapital entwickelt, in demselben Maße entwickelt sich das Proletariat, die Klasse der modernen Arbeiter, die nur so lange leben als sie Arbeit finden, und die nur so lange Arbeit finden, als ihre Arbeit das Kapital vermehrt. Diese Arbeiter, die sich stückweis verkaufen müssen, sind eine Waare wie jeder andre Handelsartikel, und daher gleichmäßig allen Wechselfällen der Konkurrenz, allen Schwankungen des Marktes ausgesetzt.

Die Arbeit der Proletarier hat durch die Ausdehnung der Maschinerie und die Theilung der Arbeit allen selbstständigen Charakter und damit allen Reiz für den Arbeiter verloren. Er wird ein bloßes Zubehör der Maschine, von dem nur der einfachste, eintönigste, am leichtesten erlernbare Handgriff verlangt wird. Die Kosten die der Arbeiter verursacht, beschränken sich daher fast nur auf die Lebensmittel, die er zu seinem Unterhalt und zur Fortpflanzung seiner Race bedarf. Der Preis einer Waare, also auch der Arbeit ist aber gleich ihren Produktionskosten. In demselben Maße, in dem die Widerwärtigkeit der Arbeit wächst, nimmt daher der Lohn ab. Noch mehr, in demselben Maße wie Maschinerie und Theilung der Arbeit zunehmen, in demselben Maße nimmt auch die Masse der Arbeit zu, sei es durch Vermehrung der Arbeitsstunden, sei es durch Vermehrung der in einer gegebenen Zeit geforderten Arbeit, beschleunigten Lauf der Maschinen u. s. w.

Die moderne Industrie hat die kleine Werkstube des patriarchalischen Meisters in die große Fabrik des industriellen Kapitalisten verwandelt. Arbeiter-

Massen in der Fabrik zusammengedrängt, werden soldatisch organisirt. Sie werden als gemeine Industriesoldaten unter die Aufsicht einer vollständigen Hierarchie von Unteroffizieren und Offizieren gestellt. Sie sind nicht nur Knechte der Bourgeoisklasse, des Bourgeoisstaates, sie sind täglich und stündlich geknechtet von der Maschine, von dem Aufseher, und vor Allem von dem einzelnen fabrizirenden Bourgeois selbst. Diese Despotie ist um so kleinlicher, gehässiger, erbitternder, je offener sie den Erwerb als ihren letzten Zweck proklamirt.

Je weniger die Handarbeit Geschicklichkeit und Kraftäußerung erheischt, d. h. je mehr die moderne Industrie sich entwickelt, desto mehr wird die Arbeit der Männer durch die der Weiber und Kinder verdrängt. Geschlechts- und Alters-Unterschiede haben keine gesellschaftliche Geltung mehr für die Arbeiterklasse. Es gibt nur noch Arbeitsinstrumente, die je nach Alter und Geschlecht verschiedene Kosten machen.

Ist die Ausbeutung des Arbeiters durch den Fabrikanten so weit beendigt, daß er seinen Arbeitslohn baar ausgezahlt erhält, so fallen die andern Theile der Bourgeoisie über ihn her, der Hausbesitzer, der Krämer, der Pfandverleiher u. s. w.

Die bisherigen kleinen Mittelstände, die kleinen Industriellen, Kaufleute und Rentiers, die Handwerker und Bauern, alle diese Klassen fallen ins Proletariat hinab, theils dadurch, das ihr kleines Kapital für den Betrieb der großen Industrie nicht ausreicht, und der Konkurrenz mit den größeren Kapitalisten erliegt, theils dadurch, daß ihre Geschicklichkeit von neuen Produktionsweisen entwerthet wird. So rekrutirt sich das Proletariat aus allen Klassen der Bevölkerung.

Das Proletariat macht verschiedene Entwicklungsstufen durch. Sein Kampf gegen die Bourgeoisie beginnt mit seiner Existenz.

Im Anfang kämpfen die einzelnen Arbeiter, dann die Arbeiter einer Fabrik, dann die Arbeiter eines Arbeitszweiges an einem Ort gegen den einzelnen Bourgeois, der sie direkt ausbeutet. Sie richten ihre Angriffe nicht nur gegen die bürgerlichen Produktions-Verhältnisse, sie richten sie gegen die Produktions-Instrumente selbst; sie vernichten die fremden konkurrirenden Waaren, sie zerschlagen die Maschinen, sie stecken die Fabriken in Brand, sie suchen sich die untergegangene Stellung des mittelalterlichen Arbeiters wieder zu erringen.

Auf dieser Stufe bilden die Arbeiter eine über das ganze Land zerstreute und durch die Konkurrenz zersplitterte Masse. Massenhafteres Zusammenhalten der Arbeiter ist noch nicht die Folge ihrer eigenen Vereinigung, sondern die Folge der Vereinigung der Bourgeoisie, die zur Erreichung ihrer eigenen politischen Zwecke das ganze Proletariat in Bewegung setzen muß und es einstweilen noch kann. Auf dieser Stufe bekämpfen die Proletarier also nicht ihre Feinde, sondern die Feinde ihrer Feinde, die Reste der absoluten Monarchie, die Grundeigenthümer, die nicht industriellen Bourgeois, die Kleinbürger. Die ganze geschichtliche Bewegung ist so in den Händen der Bourgeoisie konzentrirt; jeder Sieg, der so errungen wird, ist ein Sieg der Bourgeoisie.

Aber mit der Entwicklung der Industrie vermehrt sich nicht nur das Proletariat; es wird in größeren Massen zusammengedrängt, seine Kraft wächst und es fühlt sie mehr. Die Interessen, die Lebenslagen innerhalb des Proletariats gleichen sich immer mehr aus, indem die Maschinerie mehr und mehr die Unterschiede der Arbeit verwischt und den Lohn fast überall auf ein gleich niedriges Niveau herabdrückt. Die wachsende Konkurrenz der Bourgeois unter sich und die daraus hervorgehenden Handelskrisen machen den Lohn der Arbeiter immer schwankender; die immer rascher sich entwickelnde, unaufhörliche Verbesserung der Maschinerie macht ihre ganze Lebensstellung immer unsicherer; immer mehr nehmen die Kollisionen zwischen dem einzelnen Arbeiter und dem einzelnen Bourgeois den Charakter von Kollisionen zweier Klassen an. Die Arbeiter beginnen

labourers, crowded into the factory, are organised like soldiers. As
privates of the industrial army, they are placed under the command of
a perfect hierarchy of officers and sergeants. Not only are they
slaves of the bourgeois class, and of the bourgeois state; they are
daily and hourly enslaved by the machine, by the overlooker, and,
above all, in the individual bourgeois manufacturer himself. The more
openly this despotism proclaims gain to be its end and aim, the more
petty, the more hateful and the more embittering it is.
The less the skill and exertion of strength implied in manual labour,
in other words, the more modern industry becomes developed, the more
is the labour of men superseded by that of women. Differences of age
and sex have no longer any distinctive social validity for the working
class. All are instruments of labour, more or less expensive to use,
according to their age and sex.
No sooner is the exploitation of the labourer by the manufacturer, so
far at an end, that he receives his wages in cash, than he is set upon
by the other portion of the bourgeoisie, the landlord, the shopkeeper,
the pawnbroker, etc.
The lower strata of the middle class -- the small tradespeople,
shopkeepers, and retired tradesmen generally, the handicraftsmen and
peasants -- all these sink gradually into the proletariat, partly
because their diminutive capital does not suffice for the scale on
which Modern Industry is carried on, and is swamped in the competition
with the large capitalists, partly because their specialised skill is
rendered worthless by new methods of production. Thus, the proletariat
is recruited from all classes of the population.
The proletariat goes through various stages of development. With its
birth begins its struggle with the bourgeoisie. At first, the contest
is carried on by individual labourers, then by the work of people of a
factory, then by the operative of one trade, in one locality, against
the individual bourgeois who directly exploits them. They direct their
attacks not against the bourgeois condition of production, but against
the instruments of production themselves; they destroy imported wares
that compete with their labour, they smash to pieces machinery, they
set factories ablaze, they seek to restore by force the vanished
status of the workman of the Middle Ages.
At this stage, the labourers still form an incoherent mass scattered
over the whole country, and broken up by their mutual competition. If
anywhere they unite to form more compact bodies, this is not yet the
consequence of their own active union, but of the union of the
bourgeoisie, which class, in order to attain its own political ends,
is compelled to set the whole proletariat in motion, and is moreover
yet, for a time, able to do so. At this stage, therefore, the
proletarians do not fight their enemies, but the enemies of their
enemies, the remnants of absolute monarchy, the landowners, the
non-industrial bourgeois, the petty bourgeois. Thus, the whole
historical movement is concentrated in the hands of the bourgeoisie;
every victory so obtained is a victory for the bourgeoisie.
But with the development of industry, the proletariat not only
increases in number; it becomes concentrated in greater masses, its
strength grows, and it feels that strength more. The various interests
and conditions of life within the ranks of the proletariat are more
and more equalised, in proportion as machinery obliterates all
distinctions of labour, and nearly everywhere reduces wages to the
same low level. The growing competition among the bourgeois, and the
resulting commercial crises, make the wages of the workers ever more
fluctuating. The increasing improvement of machinery, ever more
rapidly developing, makes their livelihood more and more precarious;
the collisions between individual workmen and individual bourgeois
take more and more the character of collisions between two classes.
Thereupon, the workers begin

Back Forward Reload Stop

to form combinations (trade unions) against the bourgeois; they club together in order to keep up the rate of wages; they found permanent associations in order to make provision beforehand for these occasional revolts. Here and there, the contest breaks out into riots. Now and then the workers are victorious, but only for a time. The real fruit of their battles lie not in the immediate result, but in the ever expanding union of the workers. This union is helped on by the improved means of communication that are created by Modern Industry, and that place the workers of different localities in contact with one another. It was just this contact that was needed to centralise the numerous local struggles, all of the same character, into one national struggle between classes. But every class struggle is a political struggle. And that union, to attain which the burghers of the Middle Ages, with their miserable highways, required centuries, the modern proletarian, thanks to railways, achieve in a few years.

This organisation of the proletarians into a class, and, consequently, into a political party, is continually being upset again by the competition between the workers themselves. But it ever rises up again, stronger, firmer, mightier. It compels legislative recognition of particular interests of the workers, by taking advantage of the divisions among the bourgeoisie itself. Thus, the Ten-Hours Bill in England was carried.

Altogether, collisions between the classes of the old society further in many ways the course of development of the proletariat. The bourgeoisie finds itself involved in a constant battle. At first with the aristocracy; later on, with those portions of the bourgeoisie itself, whose interests have become antagonistic to the progress of industry; at all time with the bourgeoisie of foreign countries. In all these battles, it sees itself compelled to appeal to the proletariat, to ask for help, and thus to drag it into the political arena. The bourgeoisie itself, therefore, supplies the proletariat with its own elements of political and general education, in other words, it furnishes the proletariat with weapons for fighting the bourgeoisie.

Further, as we have already seen, entire sections of the ruling class are, by the advance of industry, precipitated into the proletariat, or are at least threatened in their conditions of existence. These also supply the proletariat with fresh elements of enlightenment and progress.

Finally, in times when the class struggle nears the decisive hour, the progress of dissolution going on within the ruling class, in fact within the whole range of old society, assumes such a violent, glaring character, that a small section of the ruling class cuts itself adrift, and joins the revolutionary class, the class that holds the future in its hands. Just as, therefore, at an earlier period, a section of the nobility went over to the bourgeoisie, so now a portion of the bourgeoisie goes over to the proletariat, and in particular, a portion of the bourgeois ideologists, who have raised themselves to the level of comprehending theoretically the historical movement as a whole.

Of all the classes that stand face to face with the bourgeoisie today, the proletariat alone is a genuinely revolutionary class. The other classes decay and finally disappear in the face of Modern Industry; the proletariat is its special and essential product.

The lower middle class, the small manufacturer, the shopkeeper, the artisan, the peasant, all these fight against the bourgeoisie, to save from extinction their existence as fractions of the middle class. They are therefore not revolutionary, but conservative. Nay, more, they are reactionary, for they try to roll back the wheel of history. If, by chance, they are revolutionary, they are only so in view of their impending transfer into the proletariat; they thus defend

damit, Coalitionen gegen die Bourgeois zu bilden; sie treten zusammen zur Behauptung ihres Arbeitslohns. Sie stiften selbst dauernde Associationen, um sich für diese gelegentlichen Empörungen zu verproviantiren. Stellenweis bricht der Kampf in Emeuten aus.

Von Zeit zu Zeit siegen die Arbeiter, aber nur vorübergehend. Das eigentliche Resultat ihrer Kämpfe ist nicht der unmittelbare Erfolg, sondern die immer weiter um sich greifende Vereinigung der Arbeiter. Sie wird befördert durch die wachsenden Kommunikationsmittel, die von der großen Industrie erzeugt werden und die Arbeiter der verschiedenen Lokalitäten mit einander in Verbindung setzen. Es bedarf aber blos der Verbindung, um die vielen Lokalkämpfe von überall gleichem Charakter, zu einem nationalen, zu einem Klassenkampf zu centralisiren. Jeder Klassenkampf aber ist ein politischer Kampf. Und die Vereinigung, zu der die Bürger des Mittelalters mit ihren Vicinalwegen Jahrhunderte bedurften, bringen die modernen Proletarier mit den Eisenbahnen in wenigen Jahren zu Stande.

Diese Organisation der Proletarier zur Klasse, und damit zur politischen Partei, wird jeden Augenblick wieder gesprengt durch die Concurrenz unter den Arbeitern selbst. Aber sie ersteht immer wieder, stärker, fester, mächtiger. Sie erzwingt die Anerkennung einzelner Interessen der Arbeiter in Gesetzesform, indem sie die Spaltungen der Bourgeoisie unter sich benutzt. So die Zehnstundenbill in England.

Die Kollisionen der alten Gesellschaft überhaupt fördern mannichfach den Entwicklungsgang des Proletariats. Die Bourgeoisie befindet sich in fortwährendem Kampf; anfangs gegen die Aristokratie; später gegen die Theile der Bourgeoisie selbst, deren Interessen mit dem Fortschritt der Industrie in Widerspruch gerathen; stets gegen die Bourgeoisie aller auswärtigen Länder. In allen diesen Kämpfen sieht sie sich genöthigt an das Proletariat zu appelliren, seine Hülfe in Anspruch zu nehmen und es so in die politische Bewegung hineinzureißen. Sie selbst führt also dem Proletariat ihre eigenen Bildungselemente, d. h. Waffen gegen sich selbst zu.

Es werden ferner, wie wir sahen, durch den Fortschritt der Industrie ganze Bestandtheile der herrschenden Klasse in's Proletariat hinabgeworfen oder wenigstens in ihren Lebensbedingungen bedroht. Auch sie führen dem Proletariat eine Masse Bildungselemente zu.

In Zeiten endlich wo der Klassenkampf sich der Entscheidung nähert, nimmt der Auflösungsprozeß innerhalb der herrschenden Klasse, innerhalb der ganzen alten Gesellschaft, einen so heftigen, so grellen Charakter an, daß ein kleiner Theil der herrschenden Klasse sich von ihr lossagt und sich der revolutionären Klasse anschließt, der Klasse, welche die Zukunft in ihren Händen trägt. Wie daher früher ein Theil des Adels zur Bourgeoisie überging, so geht jetzt ein Theil der Bourgeoisie zum Proletariat über, und namentlich ein Theil der Bourgeois-Ideologen, welche zum theoretischen Verständniß der ganzen geschichtlichen Bewegung sich hinaufgearbeitet haben.

Von allen Klassen welche heutzutage der Bourgeoisie gegenüber stehen, ist nur das Proletariat eine wirklich revolutionäre Klasse. Die übrigen Klassen verkommen und gehen unter mit der großen Industrie, das Proletariat ist ihr eigenstes Produkt.

Die Mittelstände, der kleine Industrielle, der kleine Kaufmann, der Handwerker, der Bauer, sie Alle bekämpfen die Bourgeoisie, um ihre Existenz als Mittelstände, vor dem Untergang zu sichern. Sie sind also nicht revolutionär, sondern konservativ. Noch mehr, sie sind reaktionär, denn sie suchen das Rad der Geschichte zurückzudrehen. Sind sie revolutionär, so sind sie es im Hinblick auf den ihnen bevorstehenden Uebergang ins Proletariat, so vertheidigen

sie nicht ihre gegenwärtigen, sondern ihre zukünftigen Interessen, so verla
sie ihren eigenen Standpunkt um sich auf den des Proletariats zu stellen.

Das Lumpenproletariat, diese passive Verfaulung der untersten Schich
der alten Gesellschaft, wird durch eine proletarische Revolution stellenweise
die Bewegung hineingeschleudert, seiner ganzen Lebenslage nach wird es ber
williger sein sich zu reaktionären Umtrieben erkaufen zu lassen.

Die Lebensbedingungen der alten Gesellschaft sind schon vernichtet in d
Lebensbedingungen des Proletariats. Der Proletarier ist eigenthumslos; se
Verhältniß zu Weib und Kindern hat nichts mehr gemein mit dem bürgerlich
Familienverhältniß; die moderne industrielle Arbeit, die moderne Unterjoch
unter das Kapital, dieselbe in England wie in Frankreich, in Amerika wie
Deutschland, hat ihm allen nationalen Charakter abgestreift. Die Gesetze,
Moral, die Religion sind für ihn eben so viele bürgerliche Vorurtheile, hint
denen sich eben so viele bürgerliche Interessen verstecken.

Alle früheren Klassen, die sich die Herrschaft eroberten, suchten ihre schon e
worbene Lebensstellung zu sichern, indem sie die ganze Gesellschaft den Bedi
gungen ihres Erwerbs unterwarfen. Die Proletarier können sich die gesel
schaftlichen Produktivkräfte nur erobern, indem sie ihre eigene bisherige A
eignungsweise und damit die ganze bisherige Aneignungsweise abschaffen. D
Proletarier haben Nichts von dem Ihrigen zu sichern, sie haben alle bisheri
Privatsicherheit und Privatversicherungen zu zerstören.

Alle bisherigen Bewegungen waren Bewegungen von Minoritäten oder i
Interesse von Minoritäten. Die proletarische Bewegung ist die selbstständig
Bewegung der ungeheuren Mehrzahl im Interesse der ungeheuren Mehrzah
Das Proletariat, die unterste Schichte der jetzigen Gesellschaft, kann sich nic
erheben, nicht aufrichten, ohne daß der ganze Ueberbau der Schichten, die die offi
zielle Gesellschaft bilden, in die Luft gesprengt wird.

Obgleich nicht dem Inhalt, ist der Form nach der Kampf des Proletariat
gegen die Bourgeoisie zunächst ein nationaler. Das Proletariat eines jeden Lan
des muß natürlich zuerst mit seiner eigenen Bourgeoisie fertig werden.

Indem wir die allgemeinsten Phasen der Entwicklung des Proletariats zeich
neten, verfolgten wir den mehr oder minder versteckten Bürgerkrieg innerhal
der bestehenden Gesellschaft bis zu dem Punkt, wo er in eine offene Revolution
ausbricht und durch den gewaltsamen Sturz der Bourgeoisie das Proletariat
seine Herrschaft begründet.

Alle bisherige Gesellschaft beruhte, wie wir gesehen haben, auf dem Gegensat
unterdrückender und unterdrückter Klassen. Um aber eine Klasse unterdrücken
zu können, müssen ihr Bedingungen gesichert sein innerhalb deren sie wenigstens
ihre knechtische Existenz fristen kann. Der Leibeigne hat sich zum Mitglied der
Kommune in der Leibeigenschaft herangearbeitet, wie der Kleinbürger zum Bour
geois unter dem Joch des feudalistischen Absolotismus. Der moderne Arbeiter
dagegen, statt sich mit dem Fortschritt der Industrie zu heben, sinkt immer tiefer
unter die Bedingungen seiner eignen Klasse herab. Der Arbeiter wird zum
Pauper, und der Pauperismus entwickelt sich noch rascher als Bevölkerung und
Reichthum. Es tritt hiermit offen hervor, daß die Bourgeoisie unfähig ist noch
länger die herrschende Klasse der Gesellschaft zu bleiben und die Lebensbedingungen ihrer Klasse der Gesellschaft als regelndes Gesetz aufzuzwingen. Sie
ist unfähig zu herrschen, weil sie unfähig ist ihrem Sklaven die Existenz selbst
innerhalb seiner Sklaverei zu sichern, weil sie gezwungen ist ihn in eine Lage
herabsinken zu lassen, wo sie ihn ernähren muß, statt von ihm ernährt zu werden.
Die Gesellschaft kann nicht mehr unter ihr leben, d. h. ihr Leben ist nicht mehr
verträglich mit der Gesellschft.

Die wesentlichste Bedingung für die Existenz und für die Herrschaft der Bour-

not their present, but their future interests; they desert their own
standpoint to place themselves at that of the proletariat.
The "dangerous class", the social scum, that passively rotting mass
thrown off by the lowest layers of the old society, may, here and
there, be swept into the movement by a proletarian revolution; its
conditions of life, however, prepare it far more for the part of a
bribed tool of reactionary intrigue.
In the condition of the proletariat, those of old society at large are
already virtually swamped. The proletarian is without property; his
relation to his wife and children has no longer anything in common
with the bourgeois family relations; modern industry labour, modern
subjection to capital, the same in England as in France, in America as
in Germany, has stripped him of every trace of national character.
Law, morality, religion, are to him so many bourgeois prejudices,
behind which lurk in ambush just as many bourgeois interests.
All the preceding classes that got the upper hand sought to fortify
their already acquired status by subjecting society at large to their
conditions of appropriation. The proletarians cannot become masters of
the productive forces of society, except by abolishing their own
previous mode of appropriation, and thereby also every other previous
mode of appropriation. They have nothing of their own to secure and to
fortify; their mission is to destroy all previous securities for, and
insurances of, individual property.
All previous historical movements were movements of minorities, or in
the interest of minorities. The proletarian movement is the
self-conscious, independent movement of the immense majority, in the
interest of the immense majority. The proletariat, the lowest stratum
of our present society, cannot stir, cannot raise itself up, without
the whole superincumbent strata of official society being sprung into
the air.
Though not in substance, yet in form, the struggle of the proletariat
with the bourgeoisie is at first a national struggle. The proletariat
of each country must, of course, first of all settle matters with its
own bourgeoisie.
In depicting the most general phases of the development of the
proletariat, we traced the more or less veiled civil war, raging
within existing society, up to the point where that war breaks out
into open revolution, and where the violent overthrow of the
bourgeoisie lays the foundation for the sway of the proletariat.
Hitherto, every form of society has been based, as we have already
seen, on the antagonism of oppressing and oppressed classes. But in
order to oppress a class, certain conditions must be assured to it
under which it can, at least, continue its slavish existence. The
serf, in the period of serfdom, raised himself to membership in the
commune, just as the petty bourgeois, under the yoke of the feudal
absolutism, managed to develop into a bourgeois. The modern labourer,
on the contrary, instead of rising with the process of industry, sinks
deeper and deeper below the conditions of existence of his own class.
He becomes a pauper, and pauperism develops more rapidly than
population and wealth. And here it becomes evident that the
bourgeoisie is unfit any longer to be the ruling class in society, and
to impose its conditions of existence upon society as an overriding
law. It is unfit to rule because it is incompetent to assure an
existence to its slave within his slavery, because it cannot help
letting him sink into such a state, that it has to feed him, instead
of being fed by him. Society can no longer live under this
bourgeoisie, in other words, its existence is no longer compatible
with society.
The essential conditions for the existence and for the sway of the
bour-

-geois class is the formation and augmentation of capital; the condition for capital is wage labour. Wage labour rests exclusively on competition between the labourers. The advance of industry, whose involuntary promoter is the bourgeoisie, replaces the isolation of the labourers, due to competition, by the revolutionary combination, due to association. The development of Modern Industry, therefore, cuts from under its feet the very foundation on which the bourgeoisie produces and appropriates products. What the bourgeoisie therefore produces, above all, are its own grave-diggers. Its fall and the victory of the proletariat are equally inevitable.

II.

Proletarians and Communists

In what relation do the Communists stand to the proletarians as a whole?
The Communists do not form a separate party opposed to the other working-class parties.
They have no interests separate and apart from those of the proletariat as a whole.
They do not set up any sectarian principles of their own, by which to shape and mold the proletarian movement.
The Communists are distinguished from the other working-class parties by this only: 1. In the national struggles of the proletarians of the different countries, they point out and bring to the front the common interests of the entire proletariat, independently of all nationality. 2. In the various stages of development which the struggle of the working class against the bourgeoisie has to pass through, they always and everywhere represent the interests of the movement as a whole.
The Communists, therefore, are on the one hand practically, the most advanced and resolute section of the working-class parties of every country, that section which pushes forward all others; on the other hand, theoretically, they have over the great mass of the proletariat the advantage of clearly understanding the lines of march, the conditions, and the ultimate general results of the proletarian movement.
The immediate aim of the Communists is the same as that of all other proletarian parties: Formation of the proletariat into a class, overthrow of the bourgeois supremacy, conquest of political power by the proletariat.
The theoretical conclusions of the Communists are in no way based on ideas or principles that have been invented, or discovered, by this or that would-be universal reformer.
They merely express, in general terms, actual relations springing from an existing class struggle, from a historical movement going on under our very eyes. The abolition of existing property relations is not at all a distinctive feature of communism.
All property relations in the past have continually been subject to historical change consequent upon the change in historical conditions. The French Revolution, for example, abolished feudal property in favour of bourgeois property.
The distinguishing feature of communism is not the abolition of property generally, but the abolition of bourgeois property. But modern bourgeois private property is the final and most complete expression of the system of producing and appropriating products that is based on class antagonisms, on the exploitation of the many by the few.
In this sense, the theory of the Communists may be summed up in the single sentence: Abolition of private property.

geoisklasse ist die Anhäufung des Reichthums in den Händen von Privaten, die Bildung und Vermehrung des Kapitals. Die Bedingung des Kapitals ist die Lohnarbeit. Die Lohnarbeit beruht ausschließlich auf der Konkurrenz der Arbeiter unter sich. Der Fortschritt der Industrie, dessen willenloser und widerstandsloser Träger die Bourgeoisie ist, setzt an die Stelle der Isolirung der Arbeiter durch die Konkurrenz ihre revolutionäre Vereinigung durch die Association. Mit der Entwicklung der großen Industrie wird also unter den Füßen der Bourgeoisie die Grundlage selbst weggezogen worauf sie produzirt und die Produkte sich aneignet. Sie produzirt vor Allem ihre eignen Todtengräber. Ihr Untergang und der Sieg des Proletariats sind gleich unvermeidlich.

II.
Proletarier und Kommunisten.

In welchem Verhältniß stehen die Kommunisten zu den Proletariern überhaupt?

Die Kommunisten sind keine besondere Partei gegenüber den andern Arbeiterparteien.

Sie haben keine von den Interessen des ganzen Proletariats getrennten Interessen.

Sie stellen keine besondern Prinzipien auf, wonach sie die proletarische Bewegung modeln wollen.

Die Kommunisten unterscheiden sich von den übrigen proletarischen Parteien nur dadurch, daß einerseits sie in den verschiedenen nationalen Kämpfen der Proletarier die gemeinsamen, von der Nationalität unabhängigen Interessen des gesammten Proletariats hervorheben und zur Geltung bringen, andrerseits dadurch, daß sie in den verschiedenen Entwicklungs-Stufen, welche der Kampf zwischen Proletariat und Bourgeoisie durchläuft, stets das Interesse der Gesammt-Bewegung vertreten.

Die Kommunisten sind also praktisch der entschiedenste immer weiter treibende Theil der Arbeiterparteien aller Länder, sie haben theoretisch vor der übrigen Masse des Proletariats die Einsicht in die Bedingungen, den Gang und die allgemeinen Resultate der Proletarischen Bewegung voraus.

Der nächste Zweck der Kommunisten ist derselbe wie der aller übrigen proletarischen Parteien: Bildung des Proletariats zur Klasse, Sturz der Bourgeoisieherrschaft, Eroberung der politischen Macht durch das Proletariat.

Die theoretischen Sätze der Kommunisten beruhen keineswegs auf Ideen, auf Prinzipien, die von diesem oder jenem Weltverbesserer erfunden oder entdeckt sind.

Sie sind nur allgemeine Ausdrücke thatsächlicher Verhältnisse eines existirenden Klassenkampfes, einer unter unsern Augen vor sich gehenden geschichtlichen Bewegung. Die Abschaffung bisheriger Eigenthumsverhältnisse ist nichts den Kommunismus eigenthümlich Bezeichnendes.

Alle Eigenthumsverhältnisse waren einem beständigen geschichtlichen Wechsel, einer beständigen geschichtlichen Veränderung unterworfen.

Die französische Revolution z. B. schaffte das Feudal-Eigenthum zu Gunsten des bürgerlichen ab.

Was den Kommunismus auszeichnet, ist nicht die Abschaffung des Eigenthums überhaupt, sondern die Abschaffung des bürgerlichen Eigenthums.

Aber das moderne bürgerliche Privateigenthum ist der letzte und vollendetste Ausdruck der Erzeugung und Aneignung der Producte, die auf Klassengegensätzen, die auf der Ausbeutung der Einen durch die Andern beruht.

In diesem Sinn können die Kommunisten ihre Theorie in dem einen Ausdruck: Aufhebung des Privat-Eigenthums zusammenfassen.

Man hat uns Kommunisten vorgeworfen, wir wollte: das persönlich er
bene, selbsterarbeitete Eigenthum abschaffen; das Eigenthum, welches die Gr
laze aller persönlichen Freiheit, Thätigkeit und Selbstständigkeit bilde.

Erarbeitetes, erworbenes, selbstverdientes Eigenthum! Sprecht Ihr von
kleinbürgerlichen, kleinbäuerlichen Eigenthum, welches dem bürgerlichen E
thum vorherging? Wir brauchen es nicht abzuschaffen, die Entwicklung
Industrie hat es abgeschafft und schafft es täglich ab.

Oder sprecht Ihr vom modernen bürgerlichen Privateigenthum?

Schafft aber die Lohnarbeit, die Arbeit des Proletariers ihm Eigenth
Keineswegs. Sie schafft das Kapital, d. h. das Eigenthum, welches die L
arbeit ausbeutet, welches sich nur unter der Bedingung vermehren kann, da
neue Lohnarbeit erzeugt, um sie von Neuem auszubeuten. Das Eigenthu
seiner heutigen Gestalt bewegt sich in dem Gegensaz von Kapital und L
arbeit. Betrachten wir die beiden Seiten dieses Gegensazes. Kapitalist
heißt nicht nur eine reinpersönliche, sondern eine gesellschaftliche Stellung i
Produktion einnehmen.

Das Kapital ist ein gemeinschaftliches Produkt und kann nur durch ein
meinsame Thätigkeit vieler Mitglieder, ja in letzter Instanz nur durch
gemeinsame Thätigkeit aller Mitglieder der Gesellschaft in Bewegung g
werden.

Das Kapital ist also keine persönliche, es ist eine gesellschaftliche Macht.

Wenn also das Kapital in gemeinschaftliches, allen Mitgliedern der G
schaft angehöriges Eigenthum verwandelt wird, so verwandelt sich nicht per
liches Eigenthum in gesellschaftliches. Nur der gesellschaftliche Charakter
Eigenthums verwandelt sich. Es verliert seinen Klassen-Charakter.

Kommen wir zur Lohnarbeit.

Der Durchschnittspreis der Lohnarbeit ist das Minimum des Arbeitslo
d. h. die Summe der Lebensmittel, die nothwendig sind, um den Arbeiter
Arbeiter am Leben zu erhalten. Was also der Lohnarbeiter durch seine
tigkeit sich aneignet, reicht blos dazu hin, um sein nacktes Leben wieder zu e
gen. Wir wollen diese persönliche Aneignung der Arbeitsprodukte zur L
dererzeugung des unmittelbaren Lebens keineswegs abschaffen, eine Aneign
die keine Reinertrag übrig läßt, der Macht über fremde Arbeit geben kö
Wir wollen nur den elenden Charakter dieser Aneignung aufheben, worin
Arbeiter nur lebt, um das Kapital zu vermehren, nur so weit lebt, wie es
Interesse der herrschenden Klasse erheischt.

In der bürgerlichen Gesellschaft ist die lebendige Arbeit nur ein Mittel
aufgehäufte Arbeit zu vermehren. In der kommunistischen Gesellschaft is
aufgehäufte Arbeit nur ein Mittel, um den Lebensprozeß der Arbeiter zu e
tern, zu bereichern, zu befördern.

In der bürgerlichen Gesellschaft herrscht also die Vergangenheit über die
genwart, in der kommunistischen die Gegenwart über die Vergangenheit. I
bürgerlichen Gesellschaft ist das Kapital selbstständig und persönlich, wäh
das thätige Individuum unselbstständig und unpersönlich ist.

Und die Aufhebung dieses Verhältnisses nennt die Bourgeoisie Aufheb
der Persönlichkeit und Freiheit! Und mit Recht. Es handelt sich allerdings
die Aufhebung der Bourgeois-Persönlichkeit, Selbstständigkeit und Freiheit

Unter Freiheit versteht man innerhalb der jetzigen bürgerlichen Produkti
Verhältnisse den freien Handel, den freien Kauf und Verkauf.

Fällt aber der Schacher, so fällt auch der freie Schacher. Die Redensa
vom freien Schacher, wie alle übrigen Freiheitsbravaden unserer Bourg
haben überhaupt nur einen Sinn gegenüber dem gebundenen Schacher, ge
über dem geknechteten Bürger des Mittelalters, nicht aber gegenüber der

URL: http://www.46liverpoolst.org/manifest/12.html

We Communists have been reproached with the desire of abolishing the right of personally acquiring property as the fruit of a man's own labour, which property is alleged to be the groundwork of all personal freedom, activity and independence.

Hard-won, self-acquired, self-earned property! Do you mean the property of petty artisan and of the small peasant, a form of property that preceded the bourgeois form? There is no need to abolish that; the development of industry has to a great extent already destroyed it, and is still destroying it daily.

Or do you mean the modern bourgeois private property?

But does wage labour create any property for the labourer? Not a bit. It creates capital, i.e., that kind of property which exploits wage labour, and which cannot increase except upon conditions of begetting a new supply of wage labour for fresh exploitation. Property, in its present form, is based on the antagonism of capital and wage labour. Let us examine both sides of this antagonism.

To be a capitalist, is to have not only a purely personal, but a social STATUS in production. Capital is a collective product, and only by the united action of many members, nay, in the last resort, only by the united action of all members of society, can it be set in motion. Capital is therefore not only personal; it is a social power.

When, therefore, capital is converted into common property, into the property of all members of society, personal property is not thereby transformed into social property. It is only the social character of the property that is changed. It loses its class character.

Let us now take wage labour.

The average price of wage labour is the minimum wage, i.e., that quantum of the means of subsistence which is absolutely requisite to keep the labourer in bare existence as a labourer. What, therefore, the wage labourer appropriates by means of his labour merely suffices to prolong and reproduce a bare existence. We by no means intend to abolish this personal appropriation of the products of labour, an appropriation that is made for the maintenance and reproduction of human life, and that leaves no surplus where with to command the labour of others. All that we want to do away with is the miserable character of this appropriation, under which the labourer lives merely to increase capital, and is allowed to live only in so far as the interest of the ruling class requires it.

In bourgeois society, living labour is but a means to increase accumulated labour. In communist society, accumulated labour is but a means to widen, to enrich, to promote the existence of the labourer.

In bourgeois society, therefore, the past dominates the present; in communist society, the present dominates the past. In bourgeois society, capital is independent and has individuality, while the living person is dependent and has no individuality.

And the abolition of this state of things is called by the bourgeois, abolition of individuality and freedom! And rightly so. The abolition of bourgeois individuality, bourgeois independence, and bourgeois freedom is undoubtedly aimed at.

By freedom is meant, under the present bourgeois conditions of production, free trade, free selling and buying.

But if selling and buying disappears, free selling and buying disappears also. This talk about free selling and buying, and all the other "brave words" of our bourgeois about freedom in general, have a meaning, if any, only in contrast with restricted selling and buying, with the fettered traders of the Middle Ages, but have no meaning when opposed to the com-

Back   Forward   Reload   Stop

-munist abolition of buying and selling, or the bourgeois conditions of production, and of the bourgeoisie itself.

You are horrified at our intending to do away with private property. But in your existing society, private property is already done away with for nine-tenths of the population; its existence for the few is solely due to its non-existence in the hands of those nine-tenths. You reproach us, therefore, with intending to do away with a form of property, the necessary condition for whose existence is the non-existence of any property for the immense majority of society.

In one word, you reproach us with intending to do away with your property. Precisely so; that is just what we intend.

From the moment when labour can no longer be converted into capital, money, or rent, into a social power capable of being monopolised, i.e., from the moment when individual property can no longer be transformed into bourgeois property, into capital, from that moment, you say, individuality vanishes.

You must, therefore, confess that by "individual" you mean no other person than the bourgeois, than the middle-class owner of property. This person must, indeed, be swept out of the way, and made impossible.

Communism deprives no man of the power to appropriate the products of society; all that it does is to deprive him of the power to subjugate the labour of others by means of such appropriations.

It has been objected that upon the abolition of private property, all work will cease, and universal laziness will overtake us.

According to this, bourgeois society ought long ago to have gone to the dogs through sheer idleness; for those who acquire anything, do not work. The whole of this objection is but another expression of the tautology: There can no longer be any wage labour when there is no longer any capital.

All objections urged against the communistic mode of producing and appropriating material products, have, in the same way, been urged against the communistic mode of producing and appropriating intellectual products. Just as to the bourgeois, the disappearance of class property is the disappearance of production itself, so the disappearance of class culture is to him identical with the disappearance of all culture.

That culture, the loss of which he laments, is, for the enormous majority, a mere training to act as a machine.

But don't wrangle with us so long as you apply, to our intended abolition of bourgeois property, the standard of your bourgeois notions of freedom, culture, law, etc. Your very ideas are but the outgrowth of the conditions of your bourgeois production and bourgeois property, just as your jurisprudence is but the will of your class made into a law for all, a will whose essential character and direction are determined by the economical conditions of existence of your class.

The selfish misconception that induces you to transform into eternal laws of nature and of reason the social forms stringing from your present mode of production and form of property -- historical relations that rise and disappear in the progress of production -- this misconception you share with every ruling class that has preceded you. What you see clearly in the case of ancient property, what you admit in the case of feudal property, you are of course forbidden to admit in the case of your own bourgeois form of property.

Abolition of the family! Even the most radical flare up at this infamous proposal of the Communists.

On what foundation is the present family, the bourgeois family, based? On capital, on private gain. In its completely developed form, this family exists only among the bourgeoisie. But this state of things finds its complement in the practical absence of the family among proletarians, and in public prostitution.

13

munistischen Aufhebung des Schachers, der bürgerlichen Produktions-Verhältnisse und der Bourgeoisie selbst.

Ihr entsetzt Euch darüber, daß wir das Privateigenthum aufheben wollen. Aber in Eurer bestehenden Gesellschaft ist das Privateigenthum für 9 Zehntel ihrer Mitglieder aufgehoben; es existirt gerade dadurch, daß es für 9 Zehntel nicht existirt. Ihr werft uns also vor, daß wir ein Eigenthum aufheben wollen, welches die Eigenthumslosigkeit der ungeheuren Mehrzahl der Gesellschaft als nothwendige Bedingung voraussetzt.

Ihr werft uns mit Einem Wort vor, daß wir Euer Eigenthum aufheben wollen. Allerdings das wollen wir.

Von dem Augenblick an, wo die Arbeit nicht mehr in Kapital, Geld, Grundrente, kurz, in eine monopolisirbare gesellschaftliche Macht verwandelt werden kann, d. h. von dem Augenblick, wo das persönliche Eigenthum nicht mehr in bürgerliches umschlagen kann, von dem Augenblick an erklärt Ihr die Person sei aufgehoben.

Ihr gesteht also, daß Ihr unter der Person Niemanden anders versteht, als den Bourgeois, den bürgerlichen Eigenthümer. Und diese Person soll allerdings aufgehoben werden.

Der Kommunismus nimmt keinem die Macht sich gesellschaftliche Produkte anzueignen, er nimmt nur die Macht sich durch diese Aneignung fremde Arbeit zu unterjochen.

Man hat eingewendet, mit der Aufhebung des Privateigenthums werde alle Thätigkeit aufhören und eine allgemeine Faulheit einreißen.

Hiernach müßte die bürgerliche Gesellschaft längst an der Trägheit zu Grunde gegangen sein; denn die in ihr arbeiten, erwerben nicht, und die in ihr erwerben, arbeiten nicht. Das ganze Bedenken läuft auf die Tautologie hinaus, daß es keine Lohnarbeit mehr gibt, sobald es kein Kapital mehr gibt.

Alle Einwürfe die gegen die kommunistische Aneignungs- und Produktionsweise der materiellen Produkte gerichtet werden, sind eben so auf die Aneignung und Produktion der geistigen Produkte ausgedehnt worden. Wie für den Bourgeois das Aufhören des Klasseneigenthums das Aufhören der Produktion selbst ist, so ist für ihn das Aufhören der Klassenbildung identisch mit dem Aufhören der Bildung überhaupt.

Die Bildung, deren Verlust er bedauert, ist für die enorme Mehrzahl die Heranbildung zur Maschine.

Aber streitet nicht mit uns, indem Ihr an Euren bürgerlichen Vorstellungen von Freiheit, Bildung, Recht u. s. w. die Abschaffung des bürgerlichen Eigenthums meßt. Eure Ideen selbst sind Erzeugnisse der bürgerlichen Produktions- und Eigenthums-Verhältnisse, wie Euer Recht nur der zum Gesetz erhobene Wille Eurer Klasse ist, ein Wille, dessen Inhalt gegeben ist in den materiellen Lebensbedingungen Eurer Klasse.

Die interessirte Vorstellung, worin Ihr Eure Produktions- und Eigenthumsverhältnisse aus geschichtlichen, in dem Lauf der Produktion vorübergehenden Verhältnissen in ewige Natur und Vernunftgesetze verwandelt, theilt Ihr mit allen untergegangenen herrschenden Klassen. Was Ihr für das antike Eigenthum begreift, was Ihr für das feudale Eigenthum begreift, dürft Ihr nicht mehr begreifen für das bürgerliche Eigenthum.

Aufhebung der Familie! Selbst die Radikalsten ereifern sich über diese schändliche Absicht der Kommunisten.

Worauf beruht die gegenwärtige, die bürgerliche Familie? Auf dem Kapital, auf dem Privaterwerb. Vollständig entwickelt existirt sie nur für die Bourgeoisie; aber sie findet ihre Ergänzung in der erzwungenen Familienlosigkeit der Proletarier und der öffentlichen Prostitution.

Die Familie des Bourgeois fällt natürlich weg, mit dem Wegfallen die ihrer Ergänzung und beide verschwinden mit dem Verschwinden des Kapital Werft Ihr uns vor, daß wir die Ausbeutung der Kinder durch ihre Elt aufheben wollen? Wir gestehen dies Verbrechen ein. Aber sagt Ihr, wir heben die trautesten Verhältnisse auf, indem wir an die Stelle der häuslich Erziehung die gesellschaftliche setzen.

Und ist nicht auch Eure Erziehung durch die Gesellschaft bestimmt? Dur die gesellschaftlichen Verhältnisse, innerhalb deren Ihr erzieht, durch die dir tere oder indirektere Einmischung der Gesellschaft vermittelst der Schule u. s. w. Die Kommunisten erfinden nicht die Einwirkung der Gesellschaft auf die Erzie hung; sie verändern nur ihren Charakter, sie entreißen die Erziehung dem Ei fluß einer herrschenden Klasse.

Die bürgerlichen Redensarten über Familie und Erziehung über das trau Verhältniß von Eltern und Kindern werden um so ekelhafter, je mehr in Folg der großen Industrie alle Familienbande für die Proletarier zerrissen und d Kinder in einfache Handelsartikel und Arbeitsinstrumente verwandelt werden.

Aber Ihr Kommunisten wollt die Weibergemeinschaft einführen, schreit un die ganze Bourgeoisie im Chor entgegen.

Der Bourgeois sieht in seiner Frau ein bloßes Produktions-Instrument. E hört, daß die Produktions-Instrumente gemeinschaftlich ausgebeutet werden sollen und kann sich natürlich nicht anders denken, als daß das Loos der Gemein schaftlichkeit die Weiber gleichfalls treffen wird.

Er ahnt nicht, daß es sich eben darum handelt, die Stellung der Weiber al bloßer Produktions-Instrumente aufzuheben.

Uebrigens ist nichts lächerlicher als das hochmoralische Entsetzen unsre Bourgeois über die angebliche officielle Weibergemeinschaft der Kommunisten. Die Kommunisten brauchen die Weibergemeinschaft nicht einzuführen, sie hat fa immer existirt.

Unsre Bourgeois nicht zufrieden damit, daß ihnen die Weiber und Töchter ihrer Proletarier zur Verfügung stehen, von der officiellen Prostitution gar nicht zu sprechen, finden ein Hauptvergnügen darin ihre Ehefrauen wechselseitig zu verführen.

Die bürgerliche Ehe ist in Wirklichkeit die Gemeinschaft der Ehefrauen. Man könnte höchstens den Kommunisten vorwerfen, daß sie an der Stelle einer heuch lerisch versteckten, eine officielle, offenherzige Weibergemeinschaft einführen wol len. Es versteht sich übrigens von selbst, daß mit Aufhebung der jetzigen Produktions-Verhältnisse auch die aus ihnen hervorgehende Weibergemeinschaft d. h. die officielle und nicht officielle Prostitution verschwindet.

Den Kommunisten ist ferner vorgeworfen worden, sie wollten das Vaterland, die Nationalität abschaffen.

Die Arbeiter haben kein Vaterland. Man kann ihnen nicht nehmen, was sie nicht haben. Indem das Proletariat zunächst sich die politische Herrschaft er obern, sich zur nationalen Klasse erheben, sich selbst als Nation konstituiren muß, ist es selbst noch national, wenn auch keineswegs im Sinne der Bourgeoisie.

Die nationalen Absonderungen und Gegensätze der Völker verschwinden mehr und mehr schon mit der Entwicklung der Bourgeoisie, mit der Handelsfreiheit, dem Weltmarkt, der Gleichförmigkeit der industriellen Produktion und der ihr entsprechenden Lebensverhältnisse.

Die Herrschaft des Proletariats wird sie noch mehr verschwinden machen. Vereinigte Aktion wenigstens der civilisirten Länder ist eine der ersten Bedin gungen seiner Befreiung.

In dem Maße wie die Exploitation des einen Individuums durch das andere aufgehoben wird, wird die Exploitation einer Nation durch die andre aufgehoben.

The bourgeois family will vanish as a matter of course when its complement vanishes, and both will vanish with the vanishing of capital.

Do you charge us with wanting to stop the exploitation of children by their parents? To this crime we plead guilty.

But, you will say, we destroy the most hallowed of relations, when we replace home education by social.

And your education! Is not that also social, and determined by the social conditions under which you educate, by the intervention direct or indirect, of society, by means of schools, etc.? The Communists have not intended the intervention of society in education; they do but seek to alter the character of that intervention, and to rescue education from the influence of the ruling class.

The bourgeois claptrap about the family and education, about the hallowed correlation of parents and child, becomes all the more disgusting, the more, by the action of Modern Industry, all the family ties among the proletarians are torn asunder, and their children transformed into simple articles of commerce and instruments of labour.

But you Communists would introduce community of women, screams the bourgeoisie in chorus.

The bourgeois sees his wife a mere instrument of production. He hears that the instruments of production are to be exploited in common, and, naturally, can come to no other conclusion that the lot of being common to all will likewise fall to the women.

He has not even a suspicion that the real point aimed at is to do away with the status of women as mere instruments of production.

For the rest, nothing is more ridiculous than the virtuous indignation of our bourgeois at the community of women which, they pretend, is to be openly and officially established by the Communists. The Communists have no need to introduce free love; it has existed almost from time immemorial.

Our bourgeois, not content with having wives and daughters of their proletarians at their disposal, not to speak of common prostitutes, take the greatest pleasure in seducing each other's wives. (Ah, those were the days!)

Bourgeois marriage is, in reality, a system of wives in common and thus, at the most, what the Communists might possibly be reproached with is that they desire to introduce, in substitution for a hypocritically concealed, an openly legalised system of free love. For the rest, it is self-evident that the abolition of the present system of production must bring with it the abolition of free love springing from that system, i.e., of prostitution both public and private.

The Communists are further reproached with desiring to abolish countries and nationality.

The working men have no country. We cannot take from them what they have not got. Since the proletariat must first of all acquire political supremacy, must rise to be the leading class of the nation, must constitute itself **the** nation, it is, so far, itself national, though not in the bourgeois sense of the word.

National differences and antagonism between peoples are daily more and more vanishing, owing to the development of the bourgeoisie, to freedom of commerce, to the world market, to uniformity in the mode of production and in the conditions of life corresponding thereto.

The supremacy of the proletariat will cause them to vanish still faster. United action of the leading civilised countries at least is one of the first conditions for the emancipation of the proletariat. In proportion as the exploitation of one individual by another will also be put an end to, the exploitation of one nation by another will also be put an end to.

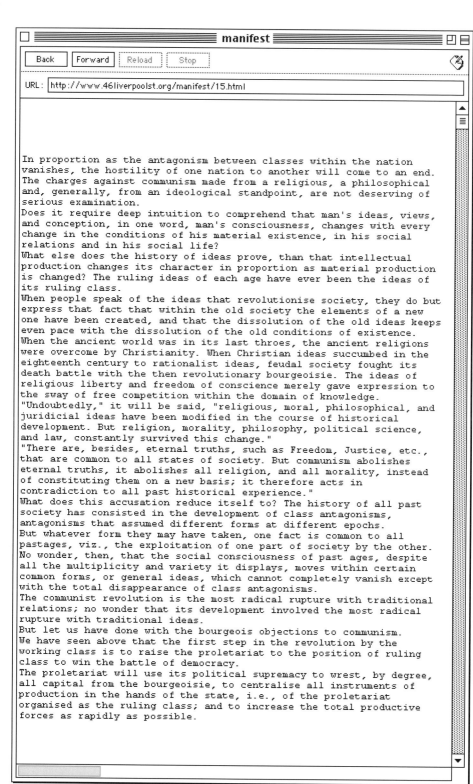

In proportion as the antagonism between classes within the nation vanishes, the hostility of one nation to another will come to an end. The charges against communism made from a religious, a philosophical and, generally, from an ideological standpoint, are not deserving of serious examination.

Does it require deep intuition to comprehend that man's ideas, views, and conception, in one word, man's consciousness, changes with every change in the conditions of his material existence, in his social relations and in his social life?

What else does the history of ideas prove, than that intellectual production changes its character in proportion as material production is changed? The ruling ideas of each age have ever been the ideas of its ruling class.

When people speak of the ideas that revolutionise society, they do but express that fact that within the old society the elements of a new one have been created, and that the dissolution of the old ideas keeps even pace with the dissolution of the old conditions of existence.

When the ancient world was in its last throes, the ancient religions were overcome by Christianity. When Christian ideas succumbed in the eighteenth century to rationalist ideas, feudal society fought its death battle with the then revolutionary bourgeoisie. The ideas of religious liberty and freedom of conscience merely gave expression to the sway of free competition within the domain of knowledge.

"Undoubtedly," it will be said, "religious, moral, philosophical, and juridicial ideas have been modified in the course of historical development. But religion, morality, philosophy, political science, and law, constantly survived this change."

"There are, besides, eternal truths, such as Freedom, Justice, etc., that are common to all states of society. But communism abolishes eternal truths, it abolishes all religion, and all morality, instead of constituting them on a new basis; it therefore acts in contradiction to all past historical experience."

What does this accusation reduce itself to? The history of all past society has consisted in the development of class antagonisms, antagonisms that assumed different forms at different epochs.

But whatever form they may have taken, one fact is common to all pastages, viz., the exploitation of one part of society by the other.

No wonder, then, that the social consciousness of past ages, despite all the multiplicity and variety it displays, moves within certain common forms, or general ideas, which cannot completely vanish except with the total disappearance of class antagonisms.

The communist revolution is the most radical rupture with traditional relations; no wonder that its development involved the most radical rupture with traditional ideas.

But let us have done with the bourgeois objections to communism.

We have seen above that the first step in the revolution by the working class is to raise the proletariat to the position of ruling class to win the battle of democracy.

The proletariat will use its political supremacy to wrest, by degree, all capital from the bourgeoisie, to centralise all instruments of production in the hands of the state, i.e., of the proletariat organised as the ruling class; and to increase the total productive forces as rapidly as possible.

Mit dem Gegensatz der Klassen im Innern der Nationen fällt die feindliche Stellung der Nationen gegen einander.

Die Anklagen gegen den Kommunismus, die von religiösen, philosophischen und ideologischen Gesichtspunkten überhaupt erhoben werden, verdienen keine ausführlichere Erörterung.

Bedarf es tiefer Einsicht um zu begreifen, daß mit den Lebensverhältnissen der Menschen, mit ihren gesellschaftlichen Beziehungen, mit ihrem gesellschaftlichen Dasein auch ihre Vorstellungen, Anschauungen und Begriffe, mit einem Worte auch ihr Bewußtsein sich ändert?

Was beweist die Geschichte der Ideen anders, als daß die geistige Produktion sich mit der materiellen umgestaltet. Die herrschenden Ideen einer Zeit waren stets nur die Ideen der herrschenden Klasse.

Man spricht von Ideen, welche eine ganze Gesellschaft revolutioniren; man spricht damit nur die Thatsache aus, daß sich innerhalb der alten Gesellschaft die Elemente einer neuen gebildet haben, daß mit der Auflösung der alten Lebensverhältnisse die Auflösung der alten Ideen gleichen Schritt hält.

Als die alte Welt im Untergehen begriffen war, wurden die alten Religionen von der christlichen Religion besiegt. Als die christlichen Ideen im 18. Jahrhundert den Aufklärungs-Ideen unterlagen, rang die feudale Gesellschaft ihren Todeskampf mit der damals revolutionären Bourgeoisie. Die Ideen der Gewissens- und Religionsfreiheit sprachen nur die Herrschaft der freien Konkurrenz auf dem Gebiet des Gewissens aus.

Aber wird man sagen, religiöse, moralische, philosophische, politische, rechtliche Ideen u. s. w. modificirten sich allerdings im Lauf der geschichtlichen Entwicklung. Die Religion, die Moral, die Philosophie, die Politik, das Recht, erhielten sich stets in diesem Wechsel.

Es gibt zudem ewige Wahrheiten wie Freiheit, Gerechtigkeit u. s. w., die allen gesellschaftlichen Zuständen gemeinsam sind. Der Kommunismus aber schafft die ewigen Wahrheiten ab, er schafft die Religion ab, die Moral, statt sie neu zu gestalten, er widerspricht also allen bisherigen geschichtlichen Entwickelungen.

Worauf reducirt sich diese Anklage? Die Geschichte der ganzen bisherigen Gesellschaft bewegte sich in Klassengegensätzen, die in den verschiedenen Epochen verschieden gestaltet waren.

Welche Form sie aber auch immer angenommen, die Ausbeutung des einen Theils der Gesellschaft durch den andern ist eine allen vergangenen Jahrhunderten gemeinsame Thatsache. Kein Wunder daher, daß das gesellschaftliche Bewußtsein aller Jahrhunderte aller Mannigfaltigkeit und Verschiedenheit zum Trotz, in gewissen gemeinsamen Formen sich bewegt, Formen, Bewußtseinsformen, die nur mit dem gänzlichen Verschwinden des Klassengegensatzes sich vollständig auflösen.

Die kommunistische Revolution ist das radikalste Brechen mit den überlieferten Eigenthums-Verhältnissen, kein Wunder, daß in ihrem Entwicklungsgange am radikalsten mit den überlieferten Ideen gebrochen wird.

Doch lassen wir die Einwürfe der Bourgeoisie gegen den Kommunismus.

Wir sahen schon oben, daß der erste Schritt in der Arbeiter-Revolution die Erhebung des Proletariats zur herrschenden Klasse, die Erkämpfung der Demokratie ist.

Das Proletariat wird seine politische Herrschaft dazu benutzen der Bourgeoisie nach und nach alles Kapital zu entreißen, alle Produktions-Instrumente in den Händen des Staats, d. h. des als herrschende Klasse organisirten Proletariats zu centralisiren und die Masse der Produktionskräfte möglichst rasch zu vermehren.

Es kann dies natürlich zunächst nur geschehen vermittelst despotischer Eingriffe in das Eigenthumsrecht und in die bürgerlichen Produktions-Verhältnisse durch Maaßregeln also, die ökonomisch unzureichend und unhaltbar erscheinen, die aber im Lauf der Bewegung über sich selbst hinaus treiben und als Mittel zur Umwälzung der ganzen Produktionsweise unvermeidlich sind.

Diese Maaßregeln werden natürlich je nach den verschiedenen Ländern verschieden sein.

Für die fortgeschrittensten Länder werden jedoch die folgenden ziemlich allgemein in Anwendung kommen können:

1) Expropriation des Grundeigenthums und Verwendung der Grundrente zu Staatsausgaben.
2) Starke Progressiv-Steuer.
3) Abschaffung des Erbrechts.
4) Konfiskation des Eigenthums aller Emigranten und Rebellen.
5) Centralisation des Kredits in den Händen des Staats durch eine Nationalbank mit Staatskapital und ausschließlichem Monopol.
6) Centralisation alles Transportwesens in den Händen des Staats.
7) Vermehrung der Nationalfabriken, Produktions-Instrumente, Urbarmachung und Verbesserung der Ländereien nach einem gemeinschaftlichen Plan.
8) Gleicher Arbeitszwang für Alle, Errichtung industrieller Armeen besonders für den Ackerbau.
9) Vereinigung des Betriebs von Ackerbau und Industrie, Hinwirken auf die allmählige Beseitigung des Gegensatzes von Stadt und Land.
10) Oeffentliche und unentgeldliche Erziehung aller Kinder. Beseitigung der Fabrikarbeit der Kinder in ihrer heutigen Form. Vereinigung der Erziehung mit der materiellen Produktion u. s. w., u. s. w.

Sind im Laufe der Entwicklung die Klassenunterschiede verschwunden, und ist alle Produktion in den Händen der associirten Individuen koncentrirt, so verliert die öffentliche Gewalt den politischen Charakter. Die politische Gewalt im eigentlichen Sinn ist die organisirte Gewalt einer Klasse zur Unterdrückung einer andern. Wenn das Proletariat im Kampfe gegen die Bourgeoisie sich nothwendig zur Klasse vereint, durch eine Revolution sich zur herrschenden Klasse macht, und als herrschende Klasse gewaltsam die alten Produktions-Verhältnisse aufhebt, so hebt es mit diesen Produktions-Verhältnissen die Existenz-Bedingungen des Klassengegensatzes der Klassen überhaupt, und damit seine eigene Herrschaft als Klasse auf.

An die Stelle der alten bürgerlichen Gesellschaft mit ihren Klassen und Klassen-Gegensätzen tritt eine Association, worin die freie Entwicklung eines Jeden, die Bedingung für die freie Entwicklung Aller ist.

III.

Socialistische und kommunistische Literatur.

1) Der reaktionaire Socialismus.

a) Der feudale Socialismus.

Die französische und englische Aristokratie war ihrer geschichtlichen Stellung nach dazu berufen, Pamphlete gegen die moderne bürgerliche Gesellschaft zu schreiben. In der französischen Julirevolution von 1830, in der englischen Reformbewegung war sie noch einmal dem verhaßten Emporkömmling erlegen. Von einem ernsten politischen Kampfe konnte nicht mehr die Rede sein. Nur der

Of course, in the beginning, this cannot be effected except by means of despotic inroads on the rights of property, and on the conditions of bourgeois production; by means of measures, therefore, which appear economically insufficient and untenable, but which, in the course of the movement, outstrip themselves, necessitate further inroads upon the old social order, and are unavoidable as a means of entirely revolutionising the mode of production.

These measures will, of course, be different in different countries. Nevertheless, in most advanced countries, the following will be pretty generally applicable:

1) Abolition of property in land and application of all rents of land to public purposes.

2) A heavy progressive or graduated income tax.

3) Abolition of all rights of inheritance.

4) Confiscation of the property of all emigrants and rebels.

5) Centralisation of credit in the banks of the state, by means of a national bank with state capital and an exclusive monopoly.

6) Centralisation of the means of communication and transport in the hands of the state.

7) Extension of factories and instruments of production owned by the state; the bringing into cultivation of waste lands, and the improvement of the soil generally in accordance with a common plan.

8) Equal obligation of all to work. Establishment of industrial armies, especially for agriculture.

9) Combination of agriculture with manufacturing industries; gradual abolition of all the distinction between town and country by a more equable distribution of the populace over the country.

10) Free education for all children in public schools. Abolition of children's factory labour in its present form. Combination of education with industrial production, etc.

When, in the course of development, class distinctions have disappeared, and all production has been concentrated in the hands of a vast association of the whole nation, the public power will lose its political character. Political power, properly so called, is merely the organised power of one class for oppressing another. If the proletariat during its contest with the bourgeoisie is compelled, by the force of circumstances, to organise itself as a class; if, by means of a revolution, it makes itself the ruling class, and, as such, sweeps away by force the old conditions of production, then it will, along with these conditions, have swept away the conditions for the existence of class antagonisms and of classes generally, and will thereby have abolished its own supremacy as a class.

In place of the old bourgeois society, with its classes and class antagonisms, we shall have an association in which the free development of each is the condition for the free development of all.

III.

Socialist and Communist Literature

1. Reactionary Socialism

a) Feudal Socialism

Owing to their historical position, it became the vocation of the aristocracies of France and England to write pamphlets against modern bourgeois society. In the French Revolution of July 1830, and in the English reform agitation, these aristocracies again succumbed to the hateful upstart. Thenceforth, a serious political struggle was altogether out of the question. A literary

battle alone remained possible. But even in the domain of literature,
the old cries of the restoration period had become impossible.
In order to arouse sympathy, the aristocracy was obliged to lose
sight, apparently, of its own interests, and to formulate its
indictment against the bourgeoisie in the interest of the exploited
working class alone. Thus, the aristocracy took their revenge by
singing lampoons on their new masters and whispering in his ears
sinister prophesies of coming catastrophe.
In this way arose feudal socialism: half lamentation, half lampoon;
half an echo of the past, half menace of the future; at times, by its
bitter, witty and incisive criticism, striking the bourgeoisie to the
very heart's core, but always ludicrous in its effect, through total
incapacity to comprehend the march of modern history.
The aristocracy, in order to rally the people to them, waved the
proletarian alms-bag in front for a banner. But the people, so often
as it joined them, saw on their hindquarters the old feudal coats of
arms, and deserted with loud and irreverent laughter.
One section of the French Legitimists and "Young England" exhibited
this spectacle.
In pointing out that their mode of exploitation was different to that
of the bourgeoisie, the feudalists forget that they exploited under
circumstances and conditions that were quite different and that are
now antiquated. In showing that, under their rule, the modern
proletariat never existed, they forget that the modern bourgeoisie is
the necessary offspring of their own form of society.
For the rest, so little do they conceal the reactionary character of
their criticism that their chief accusation against the bourgeois
amounts to this: that under the bourgeois *regime* a class is being
developed which is destined to cut up, root and branch, the old order
of society.
What they upbraid the bourgeoisie with is not so much that it creates
a proletariat as that it creates a *revolutionary* proletariat.
In political practice, therefore, they join in all corrective measures
against the working class; and in ordinary life, despite their high
falutin' phrases, they stoop to pick up the golden apples dropped from
the tree of industry, and to barter truth, love, and honour, for
traffic in wool, beetroot-sugar, and potato spirits.
As the parson has ever gone hand in hand with the landlord, so has
clerical socialism with feudal socialism.
Nothing is easier than to give Christian asceticism a socialist tinge.
Has not Christianity declaimed against private property, against
marriage, against the state? Has it not preached in the place of
these, charity and poverty, celibacy and mortification of the flesh,
monastic life and Mother Church? Christian socialism is but the holy
water with which the priest consecrates the heart-burnings of the
aristocrat.

b. Petty-Bourgeois Socialism

The feudal aristocracy was not the only class that was ruined by the
bourgeoisie, not the only class whose conditions of existence pined
and perished in the atmosphere of modern bourgeois society. The
medieval burgesses and the small peasant proprietors were the
precursors of the modern bourgeoisie. In those countries which are but
little developed, industrially and commercially, these two classes
still vegetate side by side with the rising bourgeoisie.

literarische Kampf blieb ihr übrig. Aber auch auf dem Gebiete der Literatur waren die alten Redensarten der Restaurationszeit unmöglich geworden. Um Sympathie zu erregen, mußte die Aristokratie scheinbar ihre Interessen aus den Augen verlieren und nur noch im Interesse der exploitirten Arbeiterklasse ihren Anklageakt gegen die Bourgeoisie formuliren. Sie bereitete sich so die Genugthuung vor, Schmählieder auf ihren neuen Herrscher singen und mehr oder minder unheilschwangere Prophezeihungen ihm in's Ohr raunen zu dürfen.

Auf diese Art entstand der feudalistische Socialismus, halb Klagelied, halb Pasquill, halb Rückhall der Vergangenheit, halb Dräuen der Zukunft, mitunter die Bourgeoisie in's Herz treffend durch bitteres, geistreich zerreißendes Urtheil, stets komisch wirkend durch gänzliche Unfähigkeit den Gang der modernen Geschichte zu begreifen.

Den proletarischen Bettlersack schwenkten sie als Fahne in der Hand, um das Volk hinter sich her zu versammeln. So oft es ihnen aber folgte, erblickte es auf ihrem Hintern die alten feudalen Wappen und verlief sich mit lautem und unehrerbietigem Gelächter.

Ein Theil der französischen Legitimisten und das junge England gaben dies Schauspiel zum Besten.

Wenn die Feudalen beweisen, daß ihre Weise der Ausbeutung anders gestaltet war als die bürgerliche Ausbeutung, so vergessen sie nur, daß sie unter gänzlich verschiedenen und jetzt überlebten Umständen und Bedingungen ausbeuten. Wenn sie nachweisen, daß unter ihrer Herrschaft nicht das moderne Proletariat existirt hat, so vergessen sie nur, daß eben die moderne Bourgeoisie ein nothwendiger Sprößling ihrer Gesellschaftsordnung war.

Uebrigens verheimlichen sie den reaktionären Charakter ihrer Kritik so wenig, daß ihre Hauptanklage gegen die Bourgeoisie eben darin besteht, unter ihrem Regime entwickele sich eine Klasse, welche die ganze alte Gesellschaftsordnung in die Luft sprengen werde.

Sie werfen der Bourgeoisie mehr noch vor, daß sie ein revolutionäres Proletariat, als daß sie überhaupt ein Proletariat erzeugt.

In der politischen Praxis nehmen sie daher an allen Gewaltmaßregeln gegen die Arbeiterklasse Theil, und im gewöhnlichen Leben bequemen sie sich, allen ihren aufgeblähten Redensarten zum Trotz, die goldenen Aepfel aufzulesen, und Treue, Liebe, Ehre mit dem Schacher in Schaafswolle, Runkelrüben und Schnapps zu vertauschen.

Wie der Pfaffe immer Hand in Hand ging mit dem Feudalen, so der pfäffische Socialismus mit dem feudalistischen.

Nichts leichter als dem christlichen Ascetismus einen socialistischen Anstrich zu geben. Hat das Christenthum nicht auch gegen das Privateigenthum, gegen die Ehe, gegen den Staat geeifert? Hat es nicht die Wohlthätigkeit und den Bettel, das Cölibat und die Fleischesertödtung, das Zellenleben und die Kirche an ihre Stelle gepredigt? Der heilige Socialismus ist nur das Weihwasser, womit der Pfaffe den Aerger des Aristokraten einsegnet.

b) Kleinbürgerlicher Socialismus.

Die feudale Aristokratie ist nicht die einzige Klasse, welche durch die Bourgeoisie gestürzt wurde, deren Lebensbedingungen in der modernen bürgerlichen Gesellschaft verkümmerten und abstarben. Das mittelalterliche Pfahlbürgerthum und der kleine Bauernstand waren die Vorläufer der modernen Bourgeoisie. In den weniger industriell und kommerciell entwickelten Ländern vegetirt diese Klasse noch fort neben der aufkommenden Bourgeoisie.

18

In den Ländern, wo sich die moderne Civilisation entwickelt hat, hat sich eine neue Kleinbürgerschaft gebildet, die zwischen dem Proletariat und der Bourgeoisie schwebt und als ergänzender Theil der bürgerlichen Gesellschaft stets von Neuem sich bildet, deren Mitglieder aber beständig durch die Konkurrenz in's Proletariat hinabgeschleudert werden, ja selbst mit der Entwicklung der großen Industrie einen Zeitpunkt herannahen sehen, wo sie als selbstständiger Theil der modernen Gesellschaft gänzlich verschwinden, und im Handel, in der Manufaktur, in der Agrikultur durch Arbeitsaufseher und Domestiken ersetzt werden.

In Ländern wie in Frankreich, wo die Bauernklasse weit mehr als die Hälfte der Bevölkerung ausmacht, war es natürlich, daß Schriftsteller, die für das Proletariat gegen die Bourgeoisie auftraten, an ihre Kritik des Bourgeoisregime's den kleinbürgerlichen und kleinbäuerlichen Maaßstab anlegten und die Partei der Arbeiter vom Standpunkt des Kleinbürgerthums ergriffen. Es bildete sich so der kleinbürgerliche Socialismus. Sismondi ist das Haupt dieser Literatur nicht nur für Frankreich sondern auch für England.

Dieser Socialismus zergliederte höchst scharfsinnig die Widersprüche in den modernen Produktionsverhältnissen. Er enthüllte die gleißnerischen Beschönigungen der Oekonomen. Er wies unwiderleglich die zerstörenden Wirkungen der Maschinerie und der Theilung der Arbeit nach, die Koncentration der Kapitalien und des Grundbesitzes, die Ueberproduktion, die Krisen, den nothwendigen Untergang der kleinen Bürger und Bauern, das Elend des Proletariats, die Anarchie in der Produktion, die schreienden Mißverhältnisse in der Vertheilung des Reichthums, den industriellen Vernichtungskrieg der Nationen unter einander, die Auflösung der alten Sitten, der alten Familien-Verhältnisse, der alten Nationalitäten.

Seinem positiven Gehalte nach will jedoch dieser Socialismus entweder die alten Produktions- und Verkehrsmittel wiederherstellen und mit ihnen die alten Eigenthumsverhältnisse und die alte Gesellschaft, oder er will die modernen Produktions- und Verkehrsmittel in den Rahmen der alten Eigenthumsverhältnisse, die von ihnen gesprengt werden, gesprengt werden mußten, gewaltsam wieder einsperren. In beiden Fällen ist er reaktionär und utopistisch zugleich.

Zunftwesen in der Manufaktur und patriarchalische Wirthschaft auf dem Lande, das sind seine letzten Worte.

In ihrer weitern Entwicklung hat sich diese Richtung in einen feigen Katzenjammer verlaufen.

c) Der deutsche oder der wahre Socialismus.

Die socialistische und kommunistische Literatur Frankreichs, die unter dem Druck einer herrschenden Bourgeoisie entstand und der literarische Ausdruck des Kampfs gegen diese Herrschaft ist, wurde nach Deutschland eingeführt zu einer Zeit, wo die Bourgeoisie so eben ihren Kampf gegen den feudalen Absolutismus begann.

Deutsche Philosophen, Halbphilosophen und Schöngeister bemächtigten sich gierig dieser Literatur und vergaßen nur, daß bei der Einwanderung jener Schriften aus Frankreich die französischen Lebensverhältnisse nicht gleichzeitig nach Deutschland eingewandert waren. Den deutschen Verhältnissen gegenüber verlor die französische Literatur alle unmittelbar praktische Bedeutung und nahm ein rein literarisches Aussehen an. Als müßige Spekulation über die wahre Gesellschaft, über die Verwirklichung des menschlichen Wesens mußte sie erscheinen. So hatten für die deutschen Philosophen des 18. Jahrhunderts die Forderungen der ersten französischen Revolution nur den Sinn, Forderungen der „prak

In countries where modern civilisation has become fully developed, a new class of petty bourgeois has been formed, fluctuating between proletariat and bourgeoisie, and ever renewing itself a supplementary part of bourgeois society. The individual members of this class, however, as being constantly hurled down into the proletariat by the action of competition, and, as Modern Industry develops, they even see the moment approaching when they will completely disappear as an independent section of modern society, to be replaced in manufactures, agriculture and commerce, by overlookers, bailiffs and shopmen.

In countries like France, where the peasants constitute far more than half of the population, it was natural that writers who sided with the proletariat against the bourgeoisie should use, in their criticism of the bourgeois regime, the standard of the peasant and petty bourgeois, and from the standpoint of these intermediate classes, should take up the cudgels for the working class. Thus arose petty-bourgeois socialism. Sismondi was the head of this school, not only in France but also in England.

This school of socialism dissected with great acuteness the contradictions in the conditions of modern production. It laid bare the hypocritical apologies of economists. It proved, incontrovertibly, the disastrous effects of machinery and division of labour; the concentration of capital and land in a few hands; overproduction and crises; it pointed out the inevitable ruin of the petty bourgeois and peasant, the misery of the proletariat, the anarchy in production, the crying inequalities in the distribution of wealth, the industrial war of extermination between nations, the dissolution of old moral bonds, of the old family relations, of the old nationalities.

In its positive aims, however, this form of socialism aspires either to restoring the old means of production and of exchange, and with them the old property relations, and the old society, or to cramping the modern means of production and of exchange within the framework of the old property relations that have been, and were bound to be, exploded by those means. In either case, it is both reactionary and Utopian.

Its last words are: corporate guilds for manufacture; patriarchal relations in agriculture.

Ultimately, when stubborn historical facts had dispersed all intoxicating effects of self-deception, this form of socialism ended in a miserable hangover.

c) German or 'True' Socialism

The socialist and communist literature of France, a literature that originated under the pressure of a bourgeoisie in power, and that was the expressions of the struggle against this power, was introduced into Germany at a time when the bourgeoisie in that country had just begun its contest with feudal absolutism.

German philosophers, would-be philosophers, and beaux esprits (men of letters), eagerly seized on this literature, only forgetting that when these writings immigrated from France into Germany, French social conditions had not immigrated along with them. In contact with German social conditions, this French literature lost all its immediate practical significance and assumed a purely literary aspect. Thus, to the German philosophers of the eighteenth century, the demands of the first French Revolution were nothing more than the demands of "Prac-

-tical Reason" in general, and the utterance of the will of the revolutionary French bourgeoisie signified, in their eyes, the laws of pure will, of will as it was bound to be, of true human will generally.

The work of the German *literati* consisted solely in bringing the new French ideas into harmony with their ancient philosophical conscience, or rather, in annexing the French ideas without deserting their own philosophic point of view.

This annexation took place in the same way in which a foreign language is appropriated, namely, by translation.

It is well known how the monks wrote silly lives of Catholic saints *over* the manuscripts on which the classical works of ancient heathendom had been written. The German *literati* reversed this process with the profane French literature. They wrote their philosophical nonsense beneath the French original. For instance, beneath the French criticism of the economic functions of money, they wrote 'alienation of humanity', and beneath the French criticism of the bourgeois state they wrote 'dethronement of the category of the general', and so forth.

The introduction of these philosophical phrases at the back of the French historical criticisms, they dubbed 'Philosophy of Action', 'True Socialism', 'German Science of Socialism', 'Philosophical Foundation of Socialism', and so on.

The French socialist and communist literature was thus completely emasculated. And, since it ceased, in the hands of the German, to express the struggle of one class with the other, he felt conscious of having overcome 'French one-sidedness' and of representing, not true requirements, but the requirements of truth; not the interests of the proletariat, but the interests of human nature, of man in general, who belongs to no class, has no reality, who exists only in the misty realm of philosophical fantasy.

This German socialism, which took its schoolboy task so seriously and solemnly, and extolled its poor stock-in-trade in such a mountebank fashion, meanwhile gradually lost its pedantic innocence.

The fight of the Germans, and especially of the Prussian bourgeoisie, against feudal aristocracy and absolute monarchy, in other words, the liberal movement, became more earnest.

By this, the long-wished for opportunity was offered to "True" Socialism of confronting the political movement with the socialistic demands, of hurling the traditional anathemas against liberalism, against representative government, against bourgeois competition, bourgeois freedom of the press, bourgeois legislation, bourgeois liberty and equality, and of preaching to the masses that they had nothing to gain, and everything to lose, by this bourgeois movement. German socialism forgot, in the nick of time, that the French criticism, whose silly echo it was, presupposed the existence of modern bourgeois society, with its corresponding economic conditions of existence, and the political constitution adapted thereto, the very things those attainment was the object of the pending struggle in Germany.

To the absolute governments, with their following of parsons, professors, country squires, and officials, it served as a welcome scarecrow against the threatening bourgeoisie.

It was a sweet finish, after the bitter pills of flogging and bullets, with which these same governments, just at that time, dosed the German working-class risings.

tischen Vernunft" im Allgemeinen zu sein und die Willensäußerung der revolutionären französischen Bourgeoisie bedeuteten in ihren Augen die Gesetze des reinen Willens, des Willens wie er sein muß, des wahrhaft menschlichen Willens.

Die ausschließliche Arbeit der deutschen Literaten bestand darin, die neuen französischen Ideen mit ihrem alten philosophischen Gewissen in Einklang zu setzen, oder vielmehr von ihrem philosophischen Standpunkt aus die französischen Ideen sich anzueignen.

Diese Aneignung geschah in derselben Weise, wodurch man sich überhaupt eine fremde Sprache aneignet, durch die Uebersetzung.

Es ist bekannt wie die Mönche Manuscripte, worauf die klassischen Werke der alten Heidenzeit verzeichnet waren, mit abgeschmackten katholischen Heiligengeschichten überschrieben. Die deutschen Literaten gingen umgekehrt mit der profanen französischen Literatur um. Sie schrieben ihren philosophischen Unsinn hinter das französische Original. Z. B. hinter die französische Kritik der Geldverhältnisse schrieben sie „Entäußerung des menschlichen Wesens", hinter die französische Kritik des Bourgeoisstaats schrieben sie „Aufhebung der Herrschaft des abstrakt Allgemeinen" u. s. w.

Diese Unterschiebung ihrer philosophischen Redensarten unter die französischen Entwicklungen taufte sie „Philosophie der That," „wahrer Socialismus," „Deutsche Wissenschaft des Socialismus," „Philosophische Begründung des Socialismus u. s. w.

Die französisch-socialistisch kommunistische Literatur wurde so förmlich entmannt. Und da sie in der Hand des Deutschen aufhörte, den Kampf einer Klasse gegen die andere auszudrücken, so war der Deutsche sich bewußt, die französische Einseitigkeit überwunden, statt wahrer Bedürfnisse, das Bedürfniß der Wahrheit, und statt die Interessen des Proletariers die Interessen des menschlichen Wesens, des Menschen überhaupt vertreten zu haben, des Menschen, der keiner Klasse, der überhaupt nicht der Wirklichkeit, der nur dem Dunsthimmel der philosophischen Phantasie angehört.

Dieser deutsche Socialismus, der seine unbeholfenen Schulübungen so ernst und feierlich nahm und so marktschreierisch ausposaunte, verlor indeß nach und nach seine pedantische Unschuld.

Der Kampf der deutschen namentlich der preußischen Bourgeoisie gegen die Feudalen und das absolute Königthum, mit einem Wort, die liberale Bewegung wurde ernsthafter.

Dem wahren Socialismus war so erwünschte Gelegenheit geboten, der politischen Bewegung die socialistischen Forderungen gegenüber zu stellen.

Die überlieferten Anatheme gegen den Liberalismus, gegen den Repräsentativ-Staat, gegen die bürgerliche Konkurrenz, bürgerliche Preßfreiheit, bürgerliches Recht, bürgerliche Freiheit und Gleichheit zu schleudern und der Volksmasse vorzupredigen, wie sie bei dieser bürgerlichen Bewegung nichts zu gewinnen, vielmehr Alles zu verlieren habe. Der deutsche Socialismus vergaß rechtzeitig, daß die französische Kritik, deren geistloses Echo er war, die moderne bürgerliche Gesellschaft mit den entsprechenden materiellen Lebensbedingungen und der angemessenen politischen Konstitution voraussetzt, lauter Voraussetzungen, um deren Erkämpfung es sich erst in Deutschland handelte.

Er diente den deutschen absoluten Regierungen mit ihrem Gefolge von Pfaffen, Schulmeistern, Krautjunkern und Büreaukraten als erwünschte Vogelscheuche gegen die drohend aufstrebende Bourgeoisie.

Er bildete die süßliche Ergänzung zu den bittern Peitschenhieben und Flintenkugeln, womit dieselben Regierungen die deutschen Arbeiter-Aufstände bearbeiteten.

Ward der wahre Socialismus dergestalt eine Waffe in der Hand der R
gierungen gegen die deutsche Bourgeoisie, so vertrat er auch unmittelbar e
reactionäres Interesse, das Interesse der deutschen Pfahlbürgerschaft.
Deutschland bildet das vom sechzehnten Jahrhundert her überlieferte und se
der Zeit in verschiedener Form hier immer neu wieder auftauchende Kleinbürge
thum die eigentliche gesellschaftliche Grundlage der bestehenden Zustände.

Seine Erhaltung ist die Erhaltung der bestehenden deutschen Zustände. Be
der industriellen und politischen Herrschaft der Bourgeoisie fürchtet es de
sichern Untergang, einer Seits in Folge der Koncentration des Kapitals, and
rer Seits durch das Aufkommen eines revolutionären Proletariats. D
wahre Socialismus schien ihm beide Fliegen mit einer Klappe zu schlage
Er verbreitete sich wie eine Epidemie.

Das Gewand, gewirkt aus spekulativem Spinnweb, überstickt mit schö
geistigen Redeblumen, durchtränkt von liebesschwülem Gemüthsthau, di
überschwängliche Gewand, worin die deutschen Socialisten ihre paar knöchern
ewigen Wahrheiten einhüllten, vermehrte nur den Absatz ihrer Waare b
diesem Publikum.

Seiner Seits erkannte der deutsche Socialismus immer mehr seinen Beru
der hochtrabende Vertreter dieser Pfahlbürgerschaft zu sein.

Er proklamirte die deutsche Nation als die normale Natiou und den deutsch
Spießbürger als den Normal-Menschen. Er gab jeder Niedertracht desselb
einen verborgenen höheren socialistischen Sinn, worin sie ihr Gegentheil b
deutete. Er zog die letzte Konsequenz, indem er direkt gegen die rohdestrukti
Richtung des Kommunismus auftrat, und seine unparteische Erhabenheit üb
alle Klassenkämpfe verkündete. Mit sehr wenigen Ausnahmen gehören alle
was in Deutschland von angeblich socialistischen und kommunistischen Schrifte
cirkulirt, in den Bereich dieser schmuzigen entnervenden Literatur.

2) Der konservative oder Bourgeois-Socialismus.

Ein Theil der Bourgeoisie wünscht den socialen Mißständen abzu
helfen, um den Bestand der bürgerlichen Gesellschaft zu sichern.

Es gehören hierher, Oekonomisten, Philantropen, Humanitäre, Verbesser
der Lage der arbeitenden Klassen, Wohlthätigkeits-Organisirer, Abschaffer de
Thierquälerei, Mäßigkeits-Vereinsstifter, Winkelreformer der buntscheckigste
Art. Und auch zu ganzen Systemen ist dieser Bourgeois-Socialismus aus
gearbeitet worden.

Als Beispiel führen wir Proudhon's Philosophie de la misère an.

Die socialistischen Bourgeois wollen die Lebensbedingungen der moderne
Gesellschaft ohne die nothwendig daraus hervorgehenden Kämpfe und Gefahre
Sie wollen die bestehende Gesellschaft mit Abzug der sie revolutionirenden un
sie auflösenden Elemente. Sie wollen die Bourgeoisie ohne das Proletaria
Die Bourgeoisie stellt sich die Welt, worin sie herrscht, natürlich als die bes
Welt vor. Der Bourgeois-Socialismus arbeitet diese tröstliche Vorstellun
zu einem halben oder ganzen System aus. Wenn er das Proletariat auffor
dert seine Systeme zu verwirklichen, um in das neue Jerusalem einzugehen,
verlangt er im Grunde nur, daß es in der jetzigen Gesellschaft stehen bleib
aber seine gehässigen Vorstellungen von derselben abstreife.

Eine zweite, weniger systematische und mehr praktische Form des Sociali
mus suchte der Arbeiterklasse jede revolutionäre Bewegung zu verleiden, dur
den Nachweis, wie nicht diese oder jene politische Veränderung, sondern nu
eine Veränderung der materiellen Lebensverhältnisse, der ökonomischen Ve

While this 'True' Socialism thus served the government as a weapon for fighting the German bourgeoisie, it, at the same time, directly represented a reactionary interest, the interest of German philistines. In Germany, the *petty-bourgeois* class, a relic of the sixteenth century, and since then constantly cropping up again under the various forms, is the real social basis of the existing state of things.

To preserve this class is to preserve the existing state of things in Germany. The industrial and political supremacy of the bourgeoisie threatens it with certain destruction -- on the one hand, from the concentration of capital; on the other, from the rise of a revolutionary proletariat. 'True' Socialism appeared to kill these two birds with one stone. It spread like an epidemic.

The robe of speculative cobwebs, embroidered with flowers of rhetoric, steeped in the dew of sickly sentiment, this transcendental robe in which the German Socialists wrapped their sorry 'eternal truths', all skin and bone, served to wonderfully increase the sale of their goods amongst such a public.

And on its part German socialism recognised, more and more, its own calling as the bombastic representative of the petty-bourgeois philistine.

It proclaimed the German nation to be the model nation, and the German petty philistine to be the typical man. To every villainous meanness of this model man, it gave a hidden, higher, socialistic interpretation, the exact contrary of its real character. It went to the extreme length of directly opposing the 'brutally destructive' tendency of communism, and of proclaiming its supreme and impartial contempt of all class struggles. With very few exceptions, all the so-called socialist and communist publications that now (1847) circulate in Germany belong to the domain of this foul and enervating literature.

2) Conservative or Bourgeois, Socialism

A part of the bourgeoisie is desirous of redressing social grievances in order to secure the continued existence of bourgeois society.

To this section belong economists, philanthropists, humanitarians, improvers of the condition of the working class, organisers of charity, members of societies for the prevention of cruelty to animals, temperance fanatics, hole-and-corner reformers of every imaginable kind. This form of socialism has, moreover, been worked out into complete systems.

We may cite Proudhon's *Philosophie de la Misere* as an example of this form.

The socialistic bourgeois want all the advantages of modern social conditions without the struggles and dangers necessarily resulting therefrom. They desire the existing state of society, minus its revolutionary and disintegrating elements. They wish for a bourgeoisie without a proletariat. The bourgeoisie naturally conceives the world in which it is supreme to be the best; and bourgeois socialism develops this comfortable conception into various more or less complete systems. In requiring the proletariat to carry out such a system, and thereby to march straight away into the social New Jerusalem, it but requires in reality that the proletariat should remain within the bounds of existing society, but should cast away all its hateful ideas concerning the bourgeoisie.

A second, and more practical, but less systematic, form of this socialism sought to depreciate every revolutionary movement in the eyes of the working class by showing that no mere political reform, but only a change in the material conditions of existence, in economical rel-

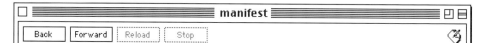

-ations, could be of any advantage to them. By changes in the material
conditions of existence, this form of socialism, however, by no means
understands abolition of the bourgeois relations of production, an
abolition that can be affected only by a revolution, but
administrative reforms, based on the continued existence of these
relations; reforms, therefore, that in no respect affect the relations
between capital and labour, but, at the best, lessen the cost, and
simplify the administrative work of bourgeois government.
Bourgeois socialism attains adequate expression when, and only when,
it becomes a mere figure of speech.
Free trade: for the benefit of the working class. Protective duties:
for the benefit of the working class. Prison reform: for the benefit
of the working class. This is the last word and the only seriously
meant word of bourgeois socialism.
It is summed up in the phrase: the bourgeois is a bourgeois -- for the
benefit of the working class.

3) Critical-Utopian Socialism and Communism

We do not here refer to that literature which, in every great modern
revolution, has always given voice to the demands of the proletariat,
such as the writings of Babeuf and others.
The first direct attempts of the proletariat to attain its own ends,
made in times of universal excitement, when feudal society was being
overthrown, necessarily failed, owing to the then undeveloped state of
the proletariat, as well as to the absence of the economic conditions
for its emancipation, conditions that had yet to be produced, and
could be produced by the impending bourgeois epoch alone. The
revolutionary literature that accompanied these first movements of the
proletariat had necessarily a reactionary character. It inculcated
universal asceticism and social levelling in its crudest form.
The socialist and communist systems, properly so called, those of
Saint-Simon, Fourier, Owen, and others, spring into existence in the
early undeveloped period, described above, of the struggle between
proletariat and bourgeoisie (see Bourgeois and Proletarians).
The founders of these systems see, indeed, the class antagonisms, as
well as the action of the decomposing elements in the prevailing form
of society. But the proletariat, as yet in its infancy, offers to them
the spectacle of a class without any historical initiative or any
independent political movement.
Since the development of class antagonism keeps even pace with the
development of industry, the economic situation, as they find it, does
not as yet offer to them the material conditions for the emancipation
of the proletariat. They therefore search after a new social science,
after new social laws, that are to create these conditions.
Historical action is to yield to their personal inventive action;
historically created conditions of emancipation to fantastic ones; and
the gradual, spontaneous class organisation of the proletariat to an
organisation of society especially contrived by these inventors.
Future history resolves itself, in their eyes, into the propaganda and
the practical carrying out of their social plans.
In the formation of their plans, they are conscious of caring chiefly
for the interests of the working class, as being the most suffering
class. Only from the point of view of being the most suffering class
does the proletariat exist for them.
The undeveloped state of the class struggle, as well as their own
surroundings, causes Socialists of this kind to consider themselves
far superior to all class antagonisms. They want to improve the
condition of every member of society, even

hältnisse ihr von Natzen sein könne. Unter Veränderung der materiellen Lebens-verhältnisse versteht dieser Socialismus aber keineswegs Abschaffung der bür-gerlichen Produktions-Verhältnisse, die nur auf revolutionärem Wege möglich ist, sondern administrative Verbesserungen, die auf dem Boden dieser Produk-tionsverhältnisse vor sich gehen; also an dem Verhältniß von Kapital und Lohnarbeit nichts ändern, sondern im besten Fall der Bourgeoisie die Kosten ihrer Herrschaft vermindern und ihren Staatshaushalt vereinfachen.

Seinen entsprechenden Ausdruck erreicht der Bourgeois-Socialismus erst da, wo er zur bloßen rednerischen Figur wird.

Freier Handel! im Interesse der arbeitenden Klasse; Schutzzölle! im Interesse der arbeitenden Klasse; Zellengefängnisse! im Interesse der arbeitenden Klasse, das ist das letzte, das einzig ernst gemeinte Wort des Bourgeois-Socialismus.

Ihr Socialismus besteht eben in der Behauptung, daß die Bourgeois Bourgeois sind—im Interesse der arbeitenden Klasse.

3) Der kritisch-utopistische Socialismus und Kommunismus.

Wir reden hier nicht von der Literatur, die in allen großen modernen Revo-lutionen die Forderungen des Proletariats aussprach (Schriften Babeufs u. s. w.).

Die ersten Versuche des Proletariats in einer Zeit allgemeiner Aufregung, in der Periode des Umsturzes der feudalen Gesellschaft direkt sein eignes Klas-seninteresse durchzusetzen, scheiterten nothwendig an der unentwickelten Gestalt des Proletariats selbst, wie an dem Mangel der materiellen Bedingungen sei-ner Befreiung, die eben erst das Produkt der bürgerlichen Epoche sind. Die revolutionäre Literatur, welche diese ersten Bewegungen des Proletariats beglei-tete, ist dem Inhalt nach nothwendig reaktionär. Sie lehrt einen allgemeinen Ascetismus und eine rohe Gleichmacherei.

Die eigentlich socialistischen und kommunistischen Systeme, die Systeme St. Simons, Fourriers, Owens u. s. w. tauchen auf in der ersten unentwickel-ten Periode des Kampfs zwischen Proletariat und Bourgeoisie, die wir oben dargestellt haben. (S. Bourgeoisie und Proletariat.)

Die Erfinder dieser Systeme sehen zwar den Gegensatz der Klassen, wie die Wirksamkeit der auflösenden Elemente in der herrschenden Gesellschaft selbst. Aber sie erblicken auf der Seite der Proletariats keine geschichtliche Selbstthätig-keit, keine ihm eigenthümliche politische Bewegung.

Da die Entwicklung des Klassengegensatzes gleichen Schritt hält mit der Entwicklung der Industrie, finden sie eben so wenig die materiellen Bedingun-gen zur Befreiung des Proletariats vor, und suchen nach einer socialen Wissen-schaft, nach socialen Gesetzen, um diese Bedingungen zu schaffen.

An die Stelle der gesellschaftlichen Thätigkeit muß ihre persönlich erfinde-rische Thätigkeit treten, an die Stelle der geschichtlichen Bedingungen der Be-freiung phantastische, an die Stelle der allmählig vor sich gehenden Organisation des Proletariats zur Klasse eine eigens ausgeheckte Organisation der Gesell-schaft. Die kommende Weltgeschichte löst sich für sie auf in die Propaganda und die praktische Ausführung ihrer Gesellschaftspläne.

Sie sind sich zwar bewußt in ihren Plänen hauptsächlich das Interesse der arbeitenden Klasse als der leidendsten Klasse zu vertreten. Nur unter diesem Gesichtspunkt der leidendsten Klasse existirt das Proletariat für sie.

Die unentwickelte Form des Klassenkampfes, wie ihre eigene Lebenslage bringen es aber mit sich, daß sie weit über jenen Klassengegensatz erhaben zu sein glauben. Sie wollen die Lebenslage aller Gesellschaftsglieder, auch ber bestgestellten verbessern. Sie appelliren daher fortwährend an die ganze Gesellschaft ohne Unterschied, ja vorzugsweise an die herrschende Klasse. Man braucht ihr System ja nur zu verstehen, um es als den bestmöglichen Plan der bestmöglichen Gesellschaft anzuerkennen.

Sie verwerfen daher alle politische, namentlich alle revolutionäre Aktion, sie wollen ihr Ziel auf friedlichem Wege erreichen und versuchen durch kleine natürlich fehlschlagende Experimente, durch die Macht des Beispiels dem neuen gesellschaftlichen Evangelium Bahn zu brechen.

Diese phantastische Schilderung der zukünftigen Gesellschaft entspricht in einer Zeit, wo das Proletariat noch höchst unentwickelt ist, also selbst noch phantastisch seine eigene Stellung auffaßt, seinem ersten ahnungsvollen Drängen nach einer allgemeinen Umgestaltung der Gesellschaft.

Die socialistischen und kommunistischen Schriften bestehen aber auch aus kritischen Elementen. Sie greifen alle Grundlagen der bestehenden Gesellschaft an. Sie haben daher höchst werthvolles Material zur Aufklärung der Arbeiter geliefert. Ihre positiven Sätze über die zukünftige Gesellschaft, z. B., Aufhebung des Gegensatzes von Stadt und Land, der Familie, des Privaterwerbs, der Lohnarbeit, die Verkündung der gesellschaftlichen Harmonie, die Verwandlung des Staats in eine bloße Verwaltung der Produktion—alle diese ihre Sätze drücken blos das Wegfallen des Klassengegensatzes aus, der eben erst sich zu entwickeln beginnt, den sie nur noch in seiner ersten gestaltlosen Unbestimmtheit kennen. Diese Sätze selbst haben daher noch einen rein utopistischen Sinn.

Die Bedeutung des kritischen utopistischen Socialismus und Kommunismus steht im umgekehrten Verhältniß zur geschichtlichen Entwicklung. In demselben Maaße, worin der Klassenkampf sich entwickelt und gestaltet, verliert diese phantastische Erhebung über denselben, diese phantastische Bekämpfung desselben, allen praktischen Werth, alle theoretische Berechtigung. Waren daher die Urheber dieser Systeme auch in vieler Beziehung revolutionär, so bilden ihre Schüler jedes Mal reaktionäre Sekten. Sie halten die alten Anschauungen der Meister fest gegenüber der geschichtlichen Fortentwicklung des Proletariats. Sie suchen daher konsequent den Klassenkampf wieder abzustumpfen und die Gegensätze zu vermitteln. Sie träumen noch immer die versuchsweise Verwirklichung ihrer gesellschaftlichen Utopien, Stiftung einzelner Phalanstere, Gründung von home-Colonien, Errichtung eines kleinen Icariens,—Duodez-Ausgabe des neuen Jerusalems—und zum Aufbau aller dieser spanischen Schlösser müssen sie an die Philantropie der bürgerlichen Herzen und Geldsäcke appelliren. Allmählig fallen sie in die Categorie der oben geschilderten reaktionären oder konservativen Socialisten, und unterscheiden sich nur mehr von ihnen durch mehr systematische Pedanterie, durch den fanatischen Aberglauben an die Wunderwirkungen ihrer socialen Wissenschaft.

Sie treten daher mit Erbitterung aller politischen Bewegung der Arbeiter entgegen, die nur aus blindem Unglauben an das neue Evangelium hervorgehen konnte.

Die Owenisten in England, die Fourieristen in Frankreich, reagiren dort gegen die Chartisten, hier gegen die Reformisten.

IV.
Stellung der Kommunisten zu den verschiedenen oppositionellen Parteien.

Nach Abschnitt 2 versteht sich das Verhältniß der Kommunisten zu den bereits konstituirten Arbeiterparteien von selbst, also ihr Verhältniß zu den Chartisten in England und den agrarischen Reformern in Nordamerika.

URL: http://www.46liverpoolst.org/manifest/22.html

that of the most favoured. Hence, they habitually appeal to society at large, without the distinction of class; nay, by preference, to the ruling class. For how can people when once they understand their system, fail to see in it the best possible plan of the best possible state of society?

Hence, they reject all political, and especially all revolutionary action; they wish to attain their ends by peaceful means, necessarily doomed to failure, and by the force of example, to pave the way for the new social gospel.

Such fantastic pictures of future society, painted at a time when the proletariat is still in a very undeveloped state and has but a fantastic conception of its own position, correspond with the first instinctive yearnings of that class for a general reconstruction of society.

But these socialist and communist publications contain also a critical element. They attack every principle of existing society. Hence, they are full of the most valuable materials for the enlightenment of the working class. The practical measures proposed in them -- such as the abolition of the distinction between town and country, of the family, of the carrying on of industries for the account of private individuals, and of the wage system, the proclamation of social harmony, the conversion of the function of the state into a more superintendence of production -- all these proposals point solely to the disappearance of class antagonisms which were, at that time, only just cropping up, and which, in these publications, are recognised in their earliest indistinct and undefined forms only. These proposals, therefore, are of a purely utopian character.

The significance of critical-utopian socialism and communism bears an inverse relation to historical development. In proportion as the modern class struggle develops and takes definite shape, this fantastic standing apart from the contest, these fantastic attacks on it, lose all practical value and all theoretical justifications. Therefore, although the originators of these systems were, in many respects, revolutionary, their disciples have, in every case, formed mere reactionary sects. They hold fast by the original views of their masters, in opposition to the progressive historical development of the proletariat. They, therefore, endeavour, and that consistently, to deaden the class struggle and to reconcile the class antagonisms. They still dream of experimental realisation of their social utopias, of founding isolated 'phalansteres', of establishing 'Home Colonies', or setting up a 'Little Icaria' -- pocket editions of the New Jerusalem -- and to realise all these castles in the air, they are compelled to appeal to the feelings and purses of the bourgeois. By degrees, they sink into the category of the reactionary conservative socialists depicted above, differing from these only by more systematic pedantry, and by their fanatical and superstitious belief in the miraculous effects of their social science.

They, therefore, violently oppose all political action on the part of the working class; such action, according to them, can only result from blind unbelief in the new gospel.

The Owenites in England, and the Fourierists in France, respectively, oppose the Chartists and the Reformistes.

IV.

Position of the Communists in Relation to the Various Existing Opposition Parties

Section 2 has made clear the relations of the Communists to the existing working-class parties, such as the Chartists in England and the Agrarian Reformers in America.

The Communists fight for the attainment of the immediate aims, for the enforcement of the momentary interests of the working class; but in the movement of the present, they also represent and take care of the future of that movement. In France, the Communists ally with the Social Democrats against the conservative and radical bourgeoisie, reserving, however, the right to take up a critical position in regard to phases and illusions traditionally handed down from the Great Revolution.

In Switzerland, they support the Radicals, without losing sight of the fact that this party consists of antagonistic elements, partly of Democratic Socialists, in the French sense, partly of radical bourgeois.

In Poland, they support the party that insists on an agrarian revolution as the prime condition for national emancipation, that party which fomented the insurrection of Krakow in 1846.

In Germany, they fight with the bourgeoisie whenever it acts in a revolutionary way, against the absolute monarchy, the feudal squirearchy, and the petty-bourgeoisie.

But they never cease, for a single instant, to instill into the working class the clearest possible recognition of the hostile antagonism between bourgeoisie and proletariat, in order that the German workers may straightway use, as so many weapons against the bourgeoisie, the social and political conditions that the bourgeoisie must necessarily introduce along with its supremacy, and in order that, after the fall of the reactionary classes in Germany, the fight against the bourgeoisie itself may immediately begin.

The Communists turn their attention chiefly to Germany, because that country is on the eve of a bourgeois revolution that is bound to be carried out under more advanced conditions of European civilisation and with a much more developed proletariat than that of England was in the seventeenth, and France in the eighteenth century, and because the bourgeois revolution in Germany will be but the prelude to an immediately following proletarian revolution.

In short, the Communists everywhere support every revolutionary movement against the existing social and political order of things.

In all these movements, they bring to the front, as the leading question in each, the property question, no matter what its degree of development at the time.

Finally, they labour everywhere for the union and agreement of the democratic parties of all countries.

The Communists disdain to conceal their views and aims. They openly declare that their ends can be attained only by the forcible overthrow of all existing social conditions. Let the ruling classes tremble at a communist revolution. The proletarians have nothing to lose but their chains. They have a world to win.

Working men of all countries, unite!

Sie kämpfen für die Erreichung der unmittelbar vorliegenden Zwecke und Interessen der Arbeiterklasse, aber sie vertreten in der gegenwärtigen Bewegung zugleich die Zukunft der Bewegung. In Frankreich schließen sich die Kommunisten an die socialistisch-demokratische Partei an gegen die konservative und radikale Bourgeoisie, ohne darum das Recht aufzugeben sich kritisch zu den aus der revolutionären Ueberlieferung herrührenden Phrasen und Illusionen zu verhalten.

In der Schweiz unterstützen sie die Radikalen, ohne zu verkennen, daß diese Partei aus widersprechenden Elementen besteht, theils aus demokratischen Socialisten im französischen Sinn, theils aus radikalen Bourgeois.

Unter den Polen unterstützen die Kommunisten die Partei, welche eine agrarische Revolution zur Bedingung der nationalen Befreiung macht. Dieselbe Partei, welche die Krakauer Insurrektion von 1846 in's Leben rief.

In Deutschland kämpft die kommunistische Partei, sobald die Bourgeoisie revolutionär auftritt, gemeinsam mit der Bourgeoisie gegen die absolute Monarchie, das feudale Grundeigenthum und die Kleinbürgerei.

Sie unterläßt aber keinen Augenblick bei den Arbeitern ein möglichst klares Bewußtsein über den feindlichen Gegensatz von Bourgeoisie und Proletariat herauszuarbeiten, damit die deutschen Arbeiter sogleich die gesellschaftlichen und politischen Bedingungen, welche die Bourgeoisie mit ihrer Herrschaft herbeiführen muß, als eben so viele Waffen gegen die Bourgeoisie kehren können, damit, nach dem Sturz der reaktionären Klassen in Deutschland, sofort der Kampf gegen die Bourgeoisie selbst beginnt.

Auf Deutschland richten die Kommunisten ihre Hauptaufmerksamkeit, weil Deutschland am Vorabend einer bürgerlichen Revolution steht, und weil es diese Umwälzung unter fortgeschritteneren Bedingungen der europäischen Civilisation überhaupt, und mit einem viel weiter entwickelten Proletariat vollbringt als England im siebenzehnten und Frankreich im achtzehnten Jahrhundert, die deutsche bürgerliche Revolution also nur das unmittelbare Vorspiel einer proletarischen Revolution sein kann.

Mit einem Wort, die Kommunisten unterstützen überall jede revolutionäre Bewegung gegen die bestehenden gesellschaftlichen und politischen Zustände.

In allen diesen Bewegungen heben sie die Eigenthumsfrage, welche mehr oder minder entwickelte Form sie auch angenommen haben möge, als die Grundfrage der Bewegung hervor.

Die Kommunisten arbeiten endlich überall an der Verbindung und Verständigung der demokratischen Parteien aller Länder.

Die Kommunisten verschmähen es, ihre Ansichten und Absichten zu verheimlichen. Sie erklären es offen, daß ihre Zwecke nur erreicht werden können durch den gewaltsamen Umsturz aller bisherigen Gesellschaftsordnung. Mögen die herrschenden Klassen vor einer Kommunistischen Revolution zittern. Die Proletarier haben nichts in ihr zu verlieren als ihre Ketten. Sie haben eine Welt zu gewinnen.

Proletarier aller Länder vereinigt Euch!

```
<!doctype HTML public "-//W3O//DTD W3 HTML 3.2//EN">
<HTML>
<HEAD>
<TITLE>The General Public License (GPL)</TITLE>
</HEAD>


<BODY TEXT="#000000" BACKGROUND=", BGCOLOR="#FFFFFF">
<center><FONT COLOR=#ff0000>GNU GENERAL PUBLIC LICENSE</FONT></center><BR>
<center>Version 2, June 1991</center><P>
Copyright (C) 1989, 1991 Free Software Foundation, Inc. 675 Mass Ave, Cambridge, MA 02139, USA.
Everyone is permitted to copy and distribute verbatim copies of this license document, but changing
it is not allowed.<p>


<center>Preamble</center><p>

The licenses for most software are designed to take away your freedom to share and change it. By
contrast, the GNU General Public License is intended to guarantee your freedom to share and change
free software--to make sure the software is free for all its users. This General Public License
applies to most of the Free Software Foundation's software and to any other program whose authors
commit to using it. (Some other Free Software Foundation software is covered by the GNU Library
General Public License instead.) You can apply it to your programs, too.<P>

When we speak of free software, we are referring to freedom, not price. Our General Public Licenses
are designed to make sure that you have the freedom to distribute copies of free software (and
charge for this service if you wish), that you receive source code or can get it if you want it,
that you can change the software or use pieces of it in new free programs; and that you know you
can do these things.<P>

To protect your rights, we need to make restrictions that forbid anyone to deny you these rights or
to ask you to surrender the rights. These restrictions translate to certain responsibilities for you
if you distribute copies of the software, or if you modify it.<P>

For example, if you distribute copies of such a program, whether gratis or for a fee, you must give
the recipients all the rights that you have. You must make sure that they, too, receive or can get
the source code. And you must show them these terms so they know their rights.<P>

We protect your rights with two steps: (1) copyright the software, and (2) offer you this license
which gives you legal permission to copy, distribute and/or modify the software.<P>

Also, for each author's protection and ours, we want to make certain that everyone understands that
there is no warranty for this free software. If the software is modified by someone else and passed
on, we want its recipients to know that what they have is not the original, so that any problems
introduced by others will not reflect on the original authors' reputations.<P>

Finally, any free program is threatened constantly by software patents. We wish to avoid the danger
that redistributors of a free program will individually obtain patent licenses, in effect making the
program proprietary. To prevent this, we have made it clear that any patent must be licensed for
everyone's free use or not licensed at all.<P>

The precise terms and conditions for copying, distribution and modification follow.<P>


<center>GNU GENERAL PUBLIC LICENSE</center>
<center>TERMS AND CONDITIONS FOR COPYING, DISTRIBUTION AND MODIFICATION</center>
<P>

0. This License applies to any program or other work which contains a notice placed by the copyright
holder saying it may be distributed under the terms of this General Public License. The "Program",
below, refers to any such program or work, and a "work based on the Program" means either the
Program or any derivative work under copyright law: that is to say, a work containing the Program or
a portion of it, either verbatim or with modifications and/or translated into another language.
(Hereinafter, translation is included without limitation in the term "modification".) Each licensee
is addressed as "you".<P>

Activities other than copying, distribution and modification are not covered by this License; they
are outside its scope. The act of running the Program is not restricted, and the output from the
Program is covered only if its contents constitute a work based on the Program (independent of hav-
ing been made by running the Program). Whether that is true depends on what the Program does.<P>

1. You may copy and distribute verbatim copies of the Program's source code as you receive it, in
any medium, provided that you conspicuously and appropriately publish on each copy an appropriate
copyright notice and disclaimer of warranty; keep intact all the notices that refer to this License
and to the absence of any warranty; and give any other recipients of the Program a copy of this
License along with the Program.<P>

You may charge a fee for the physical act of transferring a copy, and you may at your option offer
warranty protection in exchange for a fee.<P>
```